"*Two Voices* is a treasure trove of elegantly written short pieces filled with insights and good humor. It is the ideal bedside book because it can be picked up for short reading again and again."
— Robert E. Burns,
contributing editor and columnist for *U.S. Catholic*

"If you wish to discover what is possible between a father and a son, read this book. If you wish to discover what is possible in a family of faith, read this book. Or, if you simply want to see hints of wisdom built upon routine, home, life and love, read this book."
— Christopher de Vinck,
author of the Christopher Award–winning *Only the Heart Knows How to Find Them: Precious Memories for a Faithless Time*

"In *Two Voices*, a father and a son invite us into that hilarious love and prayerful work of family faith. As you read, you will hear voices in your own family. What do they say? Listening, watching—how do they show you the sacred in daily life? There is no limit. Read, and be there."
—Kim Stafford,
director, Northwest Writing Institute and
author of *Having Everything Right: Essays of Place*

"The Doyles explore Catholic life and catholic ideas with a zest and humor rare in American letters. Wrap *Two Voices* as a gift to anyone capable of seeing the angels who hover above home."
— Robin Coby,
author of the award-winning
Vogage of a Summer Sun

"Love, family, faith. What a combination Jim and Brian Doyle reveal. I laughed, I cried, I reveled in their stories of everyday life. As a father-son tandem, the Doyles are irresistable."
— Douglas Roche,
former Canadian Ambassador for
Disarmament to the U.N.

Two
Voices

TWO VOICES

A Father and Son Discuss Family and Faith

JIM DOYLE AND BRIAN DOYLE

LIGUORI
PUBLICATIONS

Liguori, Missouri

Library of Congress Cataloging-in-Publication Data

Two voices : a father and son discuss family and faith / Jim Doyle and Brian Doyle. — 1st ed.
    p.   cm.
  ISBN 0-89243-934-3 (pbk.)
    1. Doyle family. 2. Doyle, Jim, 1921- —Family. 3. Doyle, Brian, 1956- —Family. 4. United States—Biography. I. Doyle, Brian, 1956- . II Title.
CT274.D7D69 1996
929'.2'0973—dc20   96-11396

Printed in the United States of America
96 97 98 99 00 5 4 3 2 1
First Edition

Dear, near and true—take this, and pray that he,
Who wrote it, honoring your sweet faith in him,
May trust himself; and in spite of praise or scorn,
As one who feels the immeasurable world,
Attain the wise indifference of the wise;

And after Autumn past—if left to pass
His autumn into seeming-leafless days—
Draw toward the long frost and longest night,
Wearing his wisdom lightly, like the fruit
Which in our winter woodland looks a flower.

—Alfred Lord Tennyson, "A Dedication"

To Ethel
Who started it all and begat with me the boy writer
and our wonderful daughter and three other fine boys
in whom we are well pleased, and Seamus, the one who
left us early to be our family saint watching over all of
us and what we do.
Who inspires, critiques, and sustains me and my
work; who keeps the work and me honest and human;
whom I still love as much as in the old days, and will
through the long frost and longest night.
—Jim

To Mary
For her extraordinary grace and courage.
—Brian

CONTENTS

Contents

Brian:

Part 3: The Holy Roman Catholic Church   119

Brian:

Jim:

ACKNOWLEDGMENTS

Many of the essays in this volume first appeared in magazines and newspapers, and the authors are grateful to the editors and publishers of those publications for encouragement, friendship, and erudition, and for leaving our pieces pretty much alone.

All of the essays by Jim Doyle in this volume were published originally in *Catholic New York,* the newspaper of the Archdiocese of New York. We thank editor in chief Anne M. Buckley for her gracious cooperation in making them available for this book. Jim especially thanks Anne for her warm encouragement and enthusiastic support of his work, and also thanks Jerry Costello, the first editor in chief of *Catholic New York,* who initially invited him to write his column there, for his confidence.

Of Brian Doyle's essays in this volume, "Naming" appeared first in *America;* "Waiting for Lily" (under the title "The Night Watch") and "A Day with Dad" appeared in *Commonweal;* "Thoughts of Home" appeared in *Notre Dame Magazine;* "Speaking Oregon" appeared in *Oregon Quarterly;* "Two Angels" appeared in *The Critic;* "The Gaunt Man," "The Waters of Life," and "Godfathering" (as "An Offer You Can't Refuse") appeared in *U.S. Catholic;* and "Leaving" appeared in *The Oregonian.* All of his other essays in this volume were first published in the University of Portland's quarterly *Portland Magazine.* Many thanks to publisher Rev. David Tyson, C.S.C., to vice president Tony DiSpigno, and to public relations director John Soisson for much support, humor, and encouragement.

Brian Doyle wishes especially to thank Peggy Steinfels and Bob Hoyt of *Commonweal,* Revs. George Hunt and Jim Torrens of *America,* Walt Collins and Kerry Temple of *Notre Dame Magazine,* Ben Birnbaum of *Boston College Magazine,* and Tom McGrath and Cathy O'Connell-Cahill of *U.S. Catholic* for their friendship and gentle editing. Thanks too to these good friends for humor and counsel: Bob Boehmer, Lily Doyle, Mary Miller Doyle, Barry and Sandy Lopez, Lou Masson, Rev. Art Schoenfeldt, C.S.C., and Rev. Francis Sweeney, S.J.

Finally, Brian and Jim are jointly grateful to Anthony Chiffolo, our editor at Liguori, for his expert editing and patient cooperation.

INTRODUCTION

When Brian was a little boy, maybe two, he used to charm his mom and me, and other adults as well, by holding his small cup of orange juice up high, with a big smile on his face, and asking, "Won't you join me?" I'm not so sure his sister and brothers were charmed, but we were.

Now he's at it again. He has asked me to join him in this collection of essays on faith and family. It's a pleasure and honor to do so, and beyond that, a rare event, I think, for the two voices of father and son to be joined in one volume like this, fitting together so well in subject matter and concern.

Brian is our middle child. There are six years between him and his older sister and brother, but only a few years between him and his younger brothers. There are advantages and disadvantages, of course, which I will not attempt to explain, to that special position.

He is blessed with a pleasant, friendly manner and a keen wit. He makes friends easily and has hundreds of them, in high and low places. If you are one of his friends or relatives you know you are fair game to be written about, sometimes with hyperbole but always with love and beauty.

Brian has a rare and beautiful command of the language, and an awesome ability to make lovely images with words. He shows affection for his family, friends, and the world at large in the graceful, often spiritual, essays he composes—as readers of this volume will soon discover.

Having some of my essays published like this with Brian's work is a highlight of my life and career. I know my wife, his mother, Ethel Clancey Doyle, shares my joy, as she shares to a large extent in what I write, with ideas, reactions, and counsel. She also shares to a great degree in what Brian writes, having given him the right genes, excellent training, a kind and peaceful nature, and a genuine love for people.

The particular delight of this book for me is that it is Brian's first book and that I am with him in it. I predict that he will one day have lots of published books to his credit and will be a famous author. I am proud to be coauthor with him in this first one, not only because he is our boy but because he is so good at this writing business, and this is only the start of his career, of which I was a part.

—Jim

I first met Jim Doyle in the fall of 1956, when he was thirty-five years old. I have known the man now for nearly forty years, and have studied him closely, and loved him more by the year, and concluded many a time that if I might be half as gentle and wise and generous a man I would be pleased and thankful.

Some things to know about my father:

He was born in Pittsburgh and moved many times as a boy: Indiana, Ohio, Illinois. His father sold glass. He does not remember much of his childhood. The family ended up in New York City. My father wanted to be a writer. His first published story appeared in a newspaper, *The Long Island Press,* and he got five dollars for it. He was in high school. The story was about a cop.

He was president of his junior and senior classes in college. My mother was the junior class vice president from the opposing party. She ran for senior class vice president and lost because she was dating the president, whom she married in October of 1943. They have been married for fifty-three years.

My father left college in March of 1943 and joined the

U.S. Army. In the war he was in Australia, the Solomon Islands, and the Philippines. He was an expert at reading aerial photographs and translating bumps and odd structures into ammunition dumps and hidden airstrips. He was in Manila with Gen. Douglas MacArthur's forces when the atomic bomb was dropped on Hiroshima.

It was for the best, says my father.

It was also a horrible tragedy, he says.

After the war my father became an editor and promotion manager for a publishing company in New York City. He and my mother began to have children: James Aloysius III (who died when he was five months old from sudden infant death syndrome), John Kevin, Elizabeth, me, Peter. In 1962 my parents had a final son, Thomas More Patrick Doyle, and then they desisted. My brother Tom maintains that having achieved perfection as regards sons, they rested from their labors.

In 1958 my father was named the director of the Catholic Press Association of North America and Canada, a job he held for the next thirty years. As part of that job he was the writer and editor and layout man for a small newspaper called *The Catholic Journalist*. During those years my father also wrote articles and book reviews for *The Critic, View, Our Sunday Visitor*, and *U.S. Catholic*. He wrote a pamphlet called *Our Parish Council Is Alive and Working!* published by Liguori Publications (1969). By the time he retired, in 1988, he was also the American representative to the International Catholic Union of the Press and a Knight of the Order of St. Gregory the Great, appointed same by His Holiness John Paul II.

In the year that my father retired he began to write a column for *Catholic New York,* the paper of the Archdiocese of New York. He still does. His essays in this book are drawn from those columns. The essays are about the things my fathers loves and savors: children, his wife, his faith, the Church, schooling, men and women he respects, his parish, the history of the American Catholic press, books. They are also about things he does not love: evil, greed, war, and squirrels.

Like most children, I loved my parents without qualification until I was a teenager, when I began to hate them for the boundaries they placed about me; and then when I woke up from those years, at about age nineteen, I began again to love them without qualification but also with a deepening sense of the thousand ways in which they had given their lives for me, to me. Now I am nearly forty years old, and not an hour goes by in which I do not think of Jim and Ethel Doyle, who made me, who formed me, who pushed me to be a man. I love and admire them more than I can say.

—Brian

TWO
VOICES

PART I

MADONNAS
AND CHILDREN

A nd now faith, hope, and love abide, these three," wrote Paul to the Corinthians, "and the greatest of these is love." Paul knew whereof he spoke, but had he married he might have known the deep love of a subtle and wise wife: a love that may lead to peace and joy, and to the intense, hilarious, heartbreaking love with which parents embrace their children. Here then are essays about wives and daughters and sons—essays, that is, about deep and hilarious love.

WAITING FOR LILY

I am sitting in my childbirth class, carefully not watching a film. My wife is watching. I hear her gasp in horror as a French baby splashes out of a Frenchwoman. The Frenchwoman, due to the magic of cinema, has had this same baby a thousand times since the film was made in 1971. I take a quick peek between my fingers at the sole moment in the thirty-three–minute film when I do not hear light screaming from the Frenchwoman. As I do so the baby pops out with a wet sound. The doctor pulls gently, with a practiced touch, and holds the baby up to the camera. It's a girl, and we stare at each other for a moment before I cover my eyes again and she blindly gropes for her first meal.

On the way home I think about girls. The French girl in the film is now twenty, I realize, and has certainly had a little chat with her parents about her early appearance in a skin flick. Chances are that she has a lover, maybe a husband. Puberty came and went years ago. She may be finishing college. She may be working, pregnant, a mother, broken-hearted, stood up, left alone, beautiful, arrogant, gentle, in love, confused, brilliant, or dead. I think of her father, who stood dazedly by his wife, holding her hand, brushing away wet strands of hair from her forehead. He forgot to smile at the camera when his daughter was born, I noticed. The mother grinned, the doctor beamed, the nurses preened, the baby was proffered like a trophy, but the father stood there in a daze, mechanically brushing away strands of hair.

I helped my wife into bed that night, lowering her gently into place, constructing a tower of pillows around her. She fell asleep with unusual speed. In her belly our child was restless, and I watched the undulating skin, the tiny mobile mountains of my child's elbows and feet. I think it is a girl, because so many women tell us it is a boy. If it is a boy we may name him Joseph, an honest name, a name carved from wood. If it is a girl we may name her Lily, for beauty.

I watch Lily's right foot move across my wife's stomach. It courses from east to west and stops. My wife, who has grown accustomed to her restless tenant, sleeps on. Lily rolls over, her foot rippling back from west to east. I think of her feet. Now they are the size of my thumbs. In ten years they will be shod by sneakers; in twenty years they will be in high heels. I will be fifty-five years old then.

There are many nights, just now before Lily arrives, when I help my wife into bed and then sit in the dark, watching mother and daughter. I am having trouble sleeping, and sitting in the dark relaxes me. Sometimes I sit there for a couple of hours. The moon slants through the fir trees in my yard and spangles against the wall.

Lily, I want to say, Lily, I have so many things to tell you I don't know where to start. The world is so sad and so hauntingly beautiful. People are savage and holy, Lily, and nothing will hurt you as much as your lovers, and heaven is here in the love of your friends and family. There are many gods and they all have one name, which is Nameless. Your mother and I met late in life and your birth made me cry. I stood there dazed, brushing the wet hair from your mother's face. I love your mother more than I can tell you. Wisdom is in the heart and the heart is cruel. We are only people, poor and fragile. Humor is mercy. Once there was a carpenter who was dragged to the edge of a dusty town and killed; he might actually have been God. Once my mother found my brother dead. His soul remains in her heart. Touch as many things with your fingers as you can and remember them because they will pass and they are all holy. Remember me, who held you so close, so tightly; once I watched you turn in the waterworld of your mother's belly. You were not yet born. I sat in the dark and loved you until I thought my heart would break. The moon broke across the wall in splinters of silver.

I tell you this so you will know. I am a teller of stories. Stories are small prayers. I fell in love with your mother at the juncture of great waters. People are important, Lily: people. Many things are prayers: floating hawks, unfurled flags, river music, the flash of wrens in a thicket. All things pray by being themselves; evil things are empty. One of your grandfathers built a house with his hands and died within the walls he loved so. Souls are made of memory. We have seen many wars in our time. Your mother, a painter, sculpts color with her hands. Once, in a thin forest on a tiny island, a tree fell. It was an oak. I still have a piece of it. It calms me. Once I sat wrapped in the dark and waited for you. There was a moon caught in huge trees. Your mother slept, her face open and innocent, her hair cascading across her forehead. You were rolling in her belly. Your hands wrote runes on her skin. The moon wrote silver words on the wall. I waited for you. I waited for who you would be. We are only people, Lily, poor and fragile people, and we play with evil as if it were a toy. But within us are worlds without end. I waited my whole life to tell you what I cannot put into words. Once there was a moon and you danced in water and I sat in the dark and thought my heart would burst. Remember me; I held you close when you first entered the world. It was in the autumn, under a lovely silver moon.

—B.D.

Tongue Tied

My daughter, Lily, once the size of a salmon, is now the size of a wood elf. She and I are bound together in many ways. In the morning we exchange food; I ladle oatmeal into her sparrow mouth, and she carefully smears pears on my head. In the evening we dance in small circles and then we read. When we read she folds into me like a finger into a fist. On weekends I push her for miles in her stroller as she points to birds and dogs. When she sees a bird she says so, firmly, brooking no disagreement: "Bird!" When she sees a dog, however, she sits bolt upright and barks. Small dogs, I have discovered, back away uncertainly from barking infants.

We are also connected by language. Five of the words in her ten-word vocabulary are zoological: bird, duck, cat, dog, bug. These are strong words, brawny with consonants, and Lily uses them with abandon and confidence. Many times I've pointed out a wonder of the world—a hawk, an orange, my wife—and Lily has immediately and firmly identified it as a duck. She also does this when we read. We read the same four books every night, all of which feature the moon in a heroic capacity. There are also elves, singing flowers, cats in waistcoats. To Lily they are all ducks. I have tried, in my endless wisdom, to correct her—to make her say "anthropomorphic twaddle" when the whale dons his spectacles—but she sticks with duck. I use duck a good deal myself now. It's a sturdy word, strong, forthright, firm in its resolve. I admire duck.

We connect in other ways. When I come home she grins. In crowds she hides behind my legs. Sometimes, when she is tired, she staggers over to me and lies on my chest. I do not believe that a man can receive a greater compliment from his daughter.

Sometimes we just stare at each other. She will suddenly turn her laser gaze from a Cheerio and stare into my soul. Her eyes are green. I know who she is but I do not know her at all. She will be alive long after I'm dead. Not long ago she did not exist, and now she smears pears on my head. I love her more than I can tell you. She is my wife and me, and she is God's own child. She is one of the wonders of the world. She is a duck.

—B.D.

NAMING

For more than two years now I have watched my small daughter grapple with the world. She has scored victories over spoons and cups, stairs and tricycles, shirts and pants, socks and gravity. But I think her greatest accomplishment has been coming to grips with words. Two years ago she was ejected from the inland sea of her mother and thrown into a soup of incomprehensible sounds, out of which she first picked out the names of those she loves and then the names of other curiosities: cheese, crows, blackberries. I find her learning of names riveting, and watching her wrestle with words has reminded me of the startling power of names.

The issue of naming came to a head in my life when our daughter was about to be born. My wife, enormous in her eighth month, plopped into bed one night and said, gently, "Names."

We sat there silent for a moment.

"Seamus," I said, thinking of my father and grandfather and brother, all named James. My brother died when he was five months old; his nickname was Seamus, the Gaelic word for James.

"Too Irish," said my wife, gently. She knew the stories and the reasons, but she is an honest woman.

"Marie," I said.

"Too close to Mary."

"Mary."

"No way."

"Blind Lemon."

"My turn, is it?"

"Yes." We both sensed that this was a significant moment. My habit in serious moments is to furtively look for humor, which is a leavening agent and which often, unaccountably, turns solemnity into poetry and grace.

"Joseph," said my wife.

"Joseph is a very fine name. It has wood and patience in it. I like it."

"So do I."

"That's the boy, then. Girl's name?"

"Lily," she said, after a moment.

"Too flowery."

"I really like it."

"I don't. Naming your child for a flower is dorky."

"I *really* like it," said my wife, gently.

I continued to quietly dislike this name until I discovered a short poem by William Blake called "The Lilly," at which point I gave in, because Blake spoke to the angels and prophets regularly and I trust him. Also my wife is a woman of steely character, despite her elfin size. Our daughter is named Lily, and I love her name.

I do not recall that my own name has ever bothered me. Brian is uncommon but not precious, clearly of Gaelic origin but Anglicized enough to be easily spelled and pronounced, long enough to not look like a typographical error but short enough to resist diminution. There is no easy way to tack a *y* onto it, as is done so smoothly to Bob, Dan, Joe, John, Jim, and so on. In fact, there is nothing that can be done to surgically alter it; Brians are Brians, to their general satisfaction. The only exception to the sturdiness of the name I can ever recall occurred to a boyhood friend of mine who was briefly called Bri-Bri. He shed this tag, eventually, in the traditional way of boys: he punched out anyone who called him Bri-Bri. He was uniformly called Brian by the time he was twelve.

I did not actively think about my name until third grade.

One day Sister Marie Aimée asked us to file into the dimly lit library room and research the saint for whom we had been named. In my class were Anthony, James, John, Francis, Peter, Paul, Mark, Gregory, Kevin, Michael, Joseph, and Christopher. They quickly found pictures and stories of their saints in the library. So did Mary, Elizabeth, Theresa, Anne, Patricia, and Margaret. A girl named Marie was near tears for a moment until she was told that her name was a variation of Mary. She was greatly relieved and set to work writing about Mary Magdalene.

Listed under *B* were Barnabas, Barry, Bartholomew, Basil, Bathildis, Bede (the Venerable), three Benedicts, Benjamin, Berard (and Companions), Bernard, Bernardino, Bernward, Bertin, Bertrand, Bonaventure, Boniface, Brendan, and Bruno. But no Brian.

"Where is Saint Brian?" I asked the librarian.

"There is no Saint Brian."

I went home in tears. I walked from the school, named for Saint John Vianney, to my home, where my brothers Kevin, Peter, and Thomas were named for saints, where my sister, Elizabeth, was named for a saint, and where my father, James, was named for a saint. I stuttered the tale to my mother, who did not smile, for which I thank her still.

"I was not named for a saint, either," she said. This made me stop crying.

"Who were you named for, then?"

"For my mother." Their names were Ethel.

"Who was *I* named for?"

"You, my little frog, were named for a king," she said. "King Brian Boru, the first high king of Ireland. He united the clans and was the first to take up residence at Tara, the Hill of the Kings."

As a boy, as now, I was prone to visions, and I remember the vision of swirling winds and cloaks I had then, of Brian

the young king on the ramparts of his castle, of swords ring-
ing and hooves clattering, poetry chanted in the hallways,
etc. Later I discovered that Brian Boru's kingship was of a
few thousand savages thrashing about in the mud, and that
his reign lasted until he was reportedly beheaded by his brothers. I kept a sharp eye on my brothers after that.

But naming, I admit, is no laughing matter. It is easy for
me to be supercilious about those who rechristen themselves,
because I have not had to find a new name. It must be an
intolerable burden to hate your name, which is—like your
body, mind, personality, and family—something issued to you
at birth. Of those essential ingredients, names are the easiest
to change; I am told by a lawyer friend that it costs about
$150 and three weeks to legally change your name, which is
less than it would cost to remake your body or engage a psy-
chiatrist to adjust your mental image. Interestingly, you can
also change your name to anything; there are no legal restric-
tions on people labels, and you can, if you choose, name
yourself after fruit, household items, insects, crimes, types of
wood, machines, garments, or shoes.

And changing your name is a hallowed American tradition, especially among scribblers. Nathanael West, Zane Grey,
and Mark Twain, to name a few, started over whole (they
were Nathan Weinstein, Pearl Grey, and Samuel Clemens,
respectively), and among those who have edited their names
are Willa Cather (born Wilella), Henry David Thoreau (born
David Henry), Jack Kerouac (born Jean-Louis), Walt
Whitman (christened Walter), and Nathaniel Hawthorne, who
tossed a *w* in the Hathorne family name, reportedly because
he thought the extra consonant added a bit of upper crust to
the mix.

Renaming is remaking, of course. Naming yourself con-
fers autonomy, as well as the opportunity to shuck your past
and start again. It is a creation.

But there is something in changing your name that seems dishonest to me. It seems too facile. There is something slippery about it. My wife dated a man named Tom for a while. One night he told her his name wasn't Tom, and that in fact he had changed his name several times. He was fascinated with changing selves and was convinced he could slide through the American system of licenses and credit cards and identification, donning new names and faces as he chose. My wife found this chilling and broke up with him as fast as she could. He disappeared soon after, fading into the vast jungle of names. My wife is still terrified that he will show up some day, wearing a new name like an evil grin.

This story, I discover, is not uncommon. A friend told me recently of an old girlfriend of his named Tiger.

"What was her real name?"

"I don't know."

"Did she have a last name?"

"No, she was just Tiger. That was her name when I knew her. Maybe it isn't now."

Tiger is what my daughter, now two, calls her stuffed tiger. Bear is what she calls her bear. She is an aficionado of descriptive names. She often walks among the nodding fir and cedar trees of our street, naming everything she can. Names are the sounds by which she grasps trees, cousins, foods, birds. By holding their labels in her mouth, she begins to understand what they are; she begins to understand what she is to them. So naming is a chess game by which knowledge is gained and identity conferred.

We play chess, too. I move the pieces, enjoying their silent shuffle, and Lily chants their names: rook, knight, pawn, bishop, queen, king. She enjoys litanies and lists and is happy to be asked a question that will allow her to list names. There is a large photograph of her aunts and uncles and grandparents in our house. At night when I am carrying her to bed I ask her to name the people in the picture. She names everyone and concludes with her grandfather, a quiet man who may have been a saint and who ran out of breath before we met him.

His name was Bob. I like this name and often address him by it in my mind. It has an honest and direct and friendly sound. He was by all accounts an honest and direct and friendly man. When I say his name, my mouth rounds upon his honesty, the rubbery consonants framing the friendly vowel, and I feel closer to him. It is a subtle feeling but a powerful one for me. I know him only by stories, by the house he built, by the family he left, by his name. His name is a handle to the rest of what he was; his name is a way for me to believe in him.

In the very beginning of the Gospel of John, Jesus is talking to a man named Nicodemus. Either Nicodemus is dense or he is needling Christ, for he keeps asking questions of the rabbi, and Jesus keeps answering them in his patented oblique fashion. Jesus talks about the wind and the Spirit, and the manner in which grown men may be born again in the Spirit.

Nicodemus scratches his head. "How can these things be?" he asks (3:9).

Christ rambles on for a bit and then suddenly says, with great passion, that the men and women who will be saved are those who believe in his name.

This statement must have finished Nicodemus for the day— first he's told that he must be born again, and then he's instructed to believe in the name of a guy he hardly knows. I have visions of the poor man wandering home and having a long discussion with his dog about the whole matter.

But Christ's curious sentence has always intrigued me. Believe in my name and you will be saved, he says. This from a man with two working names: Jesus, the handle his parents gave him at the suggestion of an angel, and Christ, which is what everyone else called him. Not to mention the fact that he had been named long before he was born—the prophet Isaiah, for example, called him the Wonder-Counselor, God-Hero, Father-Forever, Prince of Peace. And it is ironic that, as a Jew, he was a member of a religion that refused to be so bold as to speak the name of the one true God, but instead referred to him as Yahweh, or He Who Is.

But Christ was on to something big, as usual. A name is a thing of immense power, a thing that holds soul and personality and self like a sculpted vessel. For this reason the Chinookan peoples of the Pacific Northwest had two names: one was your real name, your spirit name, and the other was your world name, the handle by which strangers could grasp you. To know the spirit name of an enemy was to possess his soul.

In our culture, much the same philosophy about names prevails. Nicknames, stage names, pen names, judicially approved new names, and the names we confer upon our children, cars, and corporations are all ways by which new entities are created. Ultimately, names are what we want things to be, no matter if those things are ourselves or the things we are trying to sell to others by means of their names. This truth is why groups like Alcoholics Anonymous place such emphasis on the admission of a problem; you cannot defeat your demon without saying its true name.

Some months ago Lily and I began to talk about God, whom she calls Gott. Usually she refers to him by name, but one night when I asked her who takes care of Lily and Momma and Daddy she thought for a moment and then smiled as sweetly and broadly as a dawn, and I suddenly realized that her smile is the true name of God, which is a word that may be said silently and that names more things than we will ever know.

—B.D.

Soul Spans

Here are some bridge stories.

Once an old man to whom I had not spoken for months although we were neighbors called me up in the middle of the night to help him pull in his beach stairs. Our houses were on the edge of the ocean and the ocean was furious. Out I went to meet him, in the slicing wind, and we pulled up his stairs, and I tore my hands, and shook his hand, and did not help him limp back to his house because he was a proud and good man, as I learned later, after we met on the bridge he had made with his words.

Once I hammered a man with my fists. This was on a muddy field long ago. We punched each other until he bled and I cried with rage and exhaustion and we were pulled apart by other men. I saw him the next day in the street. We hated each other and then he smiled. His smile was a bridge that shamed me.

Recently a friend of mine died. He was twenty-three years old. I wrote a letter to his mother about his hands, which were enormous and deft. She wrote back: a small gray card, a few quiet words, her name. The card was a bridge between despair and peace.

Recently my wife was very sick. She lay in her hospital bed like a rag. She was in a pale country far from me. I kissed her with a joke in my mouth, desperate for her smile. She smiled. The leap of her lips was a bridge between lovers.

Once, long ago, when I was a boy, I wrote a letter to my mother and left it under her plate on Mother's Day. It was a letter from Hell, refusing her admission. My father sent this letter to a small magazine, which published it and sent me a check for $10. I still have that check. It is the bridge by which I became a writer.

This morning I ate breakfast with my daughter. She is an angel with an attitude, two years old. She sat in my lap and we ate raisins. Suddenly she turned and kissed me on the nose. Her kiss was made of cinnamon and milk. The brush of her breath was a bridge to my heart.

—B.D.

LEAVING

An enormous brown box arrived at my house last week. It was a puzzle—no sign as to what might be inside and a return address I did not recognize. My daughter, Lily, and I opened it together. Lily is two years old by the calendar and a teenager by temperament.

"Do you want to help me?" I asked her.

"Bug," she said.

"It's a box. They're fun to open."

"Duck."

We opened the box. I don't know what Lily was expecting, but I was hoping for a remarkably late Christmas present from someone. Maybe cookies from Mom. Maybe a case of Irish whiskey. Maybe a tax refund so big it had to be mailed in a box the size of Idaho.

But no—it was a potty chair. The EZ-Use Relief Training Chair. Lily and I regarded it in silence. She reached out to touch the box tentatively, and then looked at me quizzically.

"Chair," I said, helpfully.

"Moon," she said, firmly, and touched the box again. She was puzzled, and so was I. What was it, exactly, that my wife and I were thinking of when we ordered this thing through the mail? The theory seemed simple and straightforward. Lily fills up her diapers all day. Diapers cost a good deal of money, and I have to write a check every month to a company called Tidee Didee. I can never write the check without laughing. Lately, Lily has become intrigued by her adventures in her diapers. Ergo, we thought, it is time to get a potty chair. The books say so.

But that careful and mature reasoning did not prepare me or my daughter for this EZ-Use Relief Training Chair, which sat, garish and stolid, in its box. Lily squatted to get a better look at it. After some minutes I placed it on the floor. We looked at it some more. Lily went and got her bear and put him in the chair. He sank out of sight, slowly, as if he were sitting in quicksand. She retrieved him and sat down in my lap, holding the bear tight. We stared at the chair some more. Neither of us spoke.

I suppose that at some point in the near future Lily will learn to use the Relief Chair. This will happen in the same slow, almost unnoticed way in which she began to sleep through the night, and go to bed without suckling at my wife's breast, and eat with her own spoon, and drink her milk from a cup. Each step along Lily's path of independence seems impossibly complex until she suddenly accomplishes it without fanfare. I am sure it will happen with this odd plastic throne. When that happens I will be happy, because it will mean the eventual cessation of diapers, and I have gotten to know the world of diapers all too well.

But I will also be saddened because it will mean another step away from me. It seems like only a few weeks ago that I met Lily for the first time—a little girl the size of a salmon, with eyes like deep black pools. She was made of stars and light. I sobbed as I carried her from the room where she was born to a nursery. I remember when she first touched my face and knew me. I remember when she first called me Dad. I remember the day when she first stumbled across the room. Now she runs from room to room, laughing. Her steps grow more confident by the day. Soon she will step away to romance, to college, to her life as a woman. I'm sure I'll be happy for her, because that is the swing and circle of life, and I am old enough to understand the paradox of possession— that what you love must leave.

But there will be a hole in me the size of a little girl, a hole that will never quite heal, a hole where she once was, the size of an elf. Today, this moment, she is two feet tall, she is an artless open kiss in the morning, she is a shout of delight in the evening, she is a poem. Eventually she will be a book, and I will love her all the more for her wisdom and grace, for the manner in which she has forged her own world. With luck I will be old then, and not dead. With luck Lily will be close, emotionally and geographically. With luck I will someday come across a huge brown box in the attic, and open it, and stare at the lurid colors of the EZ-Use Relief Training Chair, and laugh, because once I was granted the miracle of a daughter; or cry, because once I held her in my arms and that moment blazed and faded and was lost in the stream of time.

—B.D.

A Day with Dad

At four o'clock this morning, as I was walking laps around my house with my new twin sons, Liam and Joseph, on my shoulders, trying to induce the boys to belch, I noticed a car sliding backwards down our hill. Then I noticed that the hill was covered with snow. There was a great deal of snow. This is a rare event in our wet Oregon valley, and it would, I knew, shut down the town. As I watched the car slide slowly out of sight, I realized that (a) I could not get to work, (b) I could let my wife sleep, and (c) I was on duty all day.

Out of a writer's itch to record, and the need to tell the world how very bizarre a day with newborn twins can be, I decided to keep a running account of the day.

5 A.M. Still can't get over snowfall. Shocking event in our moist fir forest. Snow falling silently in gobs the size of cats. Sight reminds me of James Joyce—doesn't Joyce end a story that way? Shuffle over to the bookshelf, leaving Joseph on the couch, carting Liam under my arm. Ah, yes, "The Dead," in *Dubliners:* "…snow falling faintly through the universe and faintly falling, like the descent of their last end, upon all the living and the dead." Great ending. Liam belches—another great ending. This means he can be rolled up in his blankets like a pink cigar and stashed in the bassinet. I head for the couch to nap. Joe begins to cry. The prospect of a nap falls away faintly, faintly falling.

6 A.M. Joe still crying. He began with a whimper and built up to an operatic series of screams and wails. I put a Puccini tape on very softly; Joe likes opera and is sometimes settled by it. He simply picks up his pace and drowns out Kiri Te

Kanawa. Probably never been done before. I give up and get the bottle ready. Liam sleeping like a tree. Boy can sleep through anything. I envy him; it would be a great pleasure to have enormous hands come out of the sky and wrap me up in blankets and put me to sleep.

8 A.M. Liam sleeping like log, rock, mountain. Joe wide awake. Guzzled entire bottle in two minutes. Has not yet belched and is squirming uncomfortably. Have exhausted Puccini, Verdi, Vivaldi; am moving into jazz. Joseph doesn't like jazz much. Tough. I like jazz, and I am bigger than he is. First a little Paul Desmond, then maybe Chet Baker, then John Coltrane.

9 A.M. Joe asleep, Liam awake, their sister, Lily, age three, calling from upstairs, "Dad, I have to go to the bathroom." Construct wall of pillows around Joe on the couch and then grab Liam like a football and shuffle upstairs. On the way, pass master bedroom, tell lovely exhausted wife that she's off duty, snow falling faintly, I'm home for the day. "I love you when you're home," she says and disappears back into the blankets. Grind teeth in envy. March upstairs with Liam. Liam watching everything with interest, saying nothing. Good boy.

10 A.M. Both boys awake and yowling. Lily watching *Sesame Street,* eating a banana and two cookies for breakfast. Lily loves it when Dad makes breakfast. She is seated in a tiny rocking chair, covered with a blanket, clutching her bear. Child and bear rapt with attention. Theme song comes on; Lily sings along. Appears to know some thirty characters and actors by name. Dad resolves to write love letter to Jim Henson. Good man—made my daughter happy. Remember that Henson is dead. Resolve to pray for him, poor man. Maybe nominate him for beatification. Will write anyway— it's up to the post office to deliver the letter.

Noon. Lily eating banana and cookies for lunch. Wife in

the shower. Both boys asleep on Dad, who is still in robe and slippers. Boys arranged in such a way that Dad can with great difficulty open the sports section of the paper. Can only get to one page, though—the agate type, results of games, line-ups. Good enough. Read with interest. Results sound famil-iar—check date of paper. Ten days old. Sigh. Nothing to be done; keep reading. Mostly Oregon high school football re-sults. Hey, Klamath Falls won! Wonder where exactly Kla-math Falls is. Resolve to find out someday.

2 P.M. Shower. Bliss. Wonder what genius invented the shower. Resolve to find out someday. Stay in the shower al-most until

3 P.M. Wife feeds boys, who sprawl on the bed in milky stupor. Wife and daughter go out to play in the snow, build snowman, etc. "Boys should be asleep for quite a while," says wife. Door closes behind her with a click. Boys snap awake and stare at me. Time for Mozart—first the piano concertos, then *Don Giovanni.*

5 P.M. Joseph imitating airplane on takeoff; I put on *Don Giovanni,* he falls asleep like a stone. Brief prayer for the soul of Mozart. Great guy, died young. Had two sons, I think. Wonder what he played for them? Resolve to find out some-day. Mozart's sons remind me that Shakespeare had twins. Wonder when old Willy found time to write.

7 P.M. Dinner—yesterday's chicken, two rubbery carrots, what appears to be a zucchini, three green beans that I find in the butter drawer, a mushroom the size of my fist, butter, cream, and pasta. Steam everything in sight and then mix with the pasta. Result presentable. Thank stars for pasta. Wonder briefly who invented pasta. Think about resolving to find out but abandon the idea. Boys howling in the bed-room; upon checking, discover wife changing one and jug-gling the other. Pause in action for a kiss; wife's face so lovely and tired that I open the best bottle of wine in the house ('86

Chianti: cheeky but sincere) and put it by her plate. Lily busily eating banana and cookies for dinner.

9 P.M. Lily in bed, lovely tired wife in bed, boys asleep for the moment, lock up the house, turn out the lights, adjust the thermostat, stare out the window. It has begun to rain, and the snow is slowly sliding down the hill. Realize that I will have to go to work tomorrow. Work never seemed easier; no one cries at work. Realize with surprise that I will miss lovely funny chaos of day at home with wife and children. Realize that I love them with inarticulate, ferocious love. Realize that although I will never sleep properly again and will worry more about them all every year, they are yowling miracles beyond compare. Filled with peace and joy, briefly ponder staying up to read like a mature normal curious man of letters; get a grip on reality, resolve to get into bed and snatch a half hour of sleep, and

9:02 P.M. Do so.

—B.D.

A LOVE LETTER TO MY WIFE

As I was saying in my last letter—I love you. What does it matter if that last love letter was written nearly fifty years ago, probably one I wrote from Bougainville in the Solomons, or maybe from Manila?

Or maybe it was from Germany, when I was sent there in the Korean War. It seems I wrote you love letters only when I was far away from home, and you. Most men are like that, I guess. Distance covers the embarrassment we otherwise might feel in writing about our feelings for our wives. A love letter to one's wife? What a strange idea!

Well, I'm glad I thought to write this one now, at this very special milestone of our lives. We've been together fifty years this month—married, that is. We were also together a lot before we got married. Every day of every week, as I recall, and as much of the day as we could manage.

With the war overwhelming us like a tornado, we huddled together every minute we could, in the shelter of our love. And when we weren't together side by side, I'd telephone you a half dozen times a day, just to hear your voice and imagine your sparkling eyes warming me as we talked.

That was a very special time and kind of relationship; young love, I guess they call it. I remember the feeling: I couldn't keep my eyes off you. I admired everything about you—your wisdom, your humor, your long hair—brown, with a hint of red in it. Your smooth face, even your slightly buck teeth, your pouty lips, your great legs.

Every time I could, discreetly, I wanted to touch you, to see you, to kiss you. One old college friend says she remembers that every time I helped you on with your coat I would adjust your hair to make sure it was outside the collar. In case you didn't know: it was just a ploy to touch you again.

Just your walking into a room gave a kick to my libido. I was jealous, even of our friends when you were talking with them. I wanted you all for myself all the time. And that, of course, is what marriage is—a contract that says we give ourselves fully to each other, and we have each other forever in this life and after.

Nothing much has changed over these years, except us. Our bodies are older, larger, less agile. Our hair color is different, and our skin not so smooth. But the way we feel about each other is pretty much the same, though we're wiser and surer of each other and our love.

Renewing our marriage vows last week at our Fiftieth Anniversary Mass of Thanksgiving, with all our family and friends in the church, reminded me of that: our commitment so long ago, and now again, to love and honor each other always, in the good times and bad, in sickness and health.

Along the way in this half century we've had our sadnesses, our joys, our sicknesses and recoveries, our failures and successes, our separations and our reunions—as everyone does. Somehow, we have been allowed to survive it all and stay together.

We have to ask ourselves, and especially God, why we have been so blessed, when so many men we know have lost their wives to death, and so many women have lost their husbands. That must surely be the greatest pain of all, and what follows the greatest loneliness one can ever suffer, and to carry on the greatest expression of faith and courage one can imagine.

When others have been separated by divorce, by illness of body or sickness of spirit, why were we allowed to survive together these fifty years? Why, Lord? It surely is a mystery and—in the words of the final song we selected for our Thanksgiving Mass—an amazing grace.

A poet of the late nineteenth century, Richard Garnett, wrote, "Man and Woman may only enter Paradise hand in hand. Together, the myth tells us they left it, and together they must return." For those who have loved for so many years, it seems the right and proper thing to do.

—J.D.

A Few Hours to Yourself

There's that ancient one-liner about a wife who says she married her husband—who's retiring—for better or worse, for richer or poorer, but not for lunch. There's some truth to that, I guess, but my wife and I—now that we are retired—usually do have lunch together. Not to mention breakfast and dinner as well.

Togetherness, however, is something to be enjoyed in moderation, like food, drink, and exercise. We've discovered that it's also essential for each of us to have some hours alone, from time to time, if we are to be happy and continue loving each other in our years as senior citizens, as government agencies and people trying to sell us something insist on calling us.

We're together most of every day, of course, doing this and that and going here and there. We manage to get to Mass nearly every day, we go shopping, and we work around the house and garden together. (She makes the big landscaping and repair decisions, of course, and I execute them, doing the digging, the fixing, and the painting.)

Even though retired and with no office we need to go to, we keep busy enough to be able to say, as we do, that we've never been busier. We're as busy as always but with different things we want to do, going in new directions, following new goals.

And, thank God, we are still able to do a lot of traveling together. We're on the road quite a bit (like Charles Kuralt), only we are visiting our children and grandchildren in New York, Oregon, Chicago, or Colorado. Or we're visiting friends elsewhere.

Occasionally, having saved up our dollars, we set out on a longer, more ambitious trip, such as the one we recently made to visit old friends in Germany and then to see Paris and London for the first time.

In what passes for our normal week, however, we each have several blocks of time scattered across different days when we do things alone. Without ever talking about it or agreeing to do it, it seems, we've worked out a system of separating now and then so that we are not in each other's way, and ears, all the time. We think we are the better for it. Such a time alone makes coming together again a new small pleasure.

Ethel is part of the Literacy Volunteers of America and teaches a young man to read, two days a week, and she spends a good part of another day staffing the parish human-services outreach office. I go off by myself to play golf a couple of days, and tennis one evening, and I retreat here to the word processor nearly every day for some writing. When I'm here alone, though, I can still hear her banging away on her clattering old typewriter in another room.

Because each of us has private interests we follow from time to time, we find our lunches and dinners together are more occasions for sharing ideas we've had, plans we want to propose, or suggestions for trips we'd like to make. Even breakfast has become a time to exchange going-to-sleep or waking-up thoughts that suddenly appeared in the dark.

Yes, we senior couples—who are in what the French call the third age—who have been together so long and know each other so well, need to seek some privacy, that "obscure nook for me," as Robert Browning called it. Too much togetherness can be oppressive, leading to irritation and carping. We older types need our own personal time and space, as our junior citizens are fond of saying.

Come to think of it, though, Ethel's been gone a real long time this afternoon. She's out doing her stint with parish human services, and then she had a doctor's appointment. I wonder what's keeping her so long, and what the doctor had to say. It sure is quiet and lonely here.

—J.D.

THE OLD FAMILY DOLLHOUSE

We have just discovered a family heirloom hidden in our basement. It might be more accurate to say we have unearthed it, because we had to release it from lots of other old things piled on top of it. It is an old handmade dollhouse, which we are now in the process of repairing and refurbishing.

This dollhouse was built by my wife's grandfather, Richard McCluskey, a roofer by trade from St. Brigid's Parish on Avenue B in Manhattan. He made it for Ethel when she was a little girl.

Ethel played with it when she and her family lived up in Pelham. When she was too old for it, her father, John Clancey, fixed it up again, and her sister, Betty, played with it for a few years. When Ethel's father died and her mother broke up their home and came to live with us, the dollhouse came along.

Our daughter, Betsy, played with it when she was little, and then our three youngest sons attacked it, in their special way of playing, and the dollhouse, somewhat beaten, has lain in our basement ever since. It's been down there twenty years or more—unplayed with, unwanted, so covered over with other good stuff not ready yet to be discarded that I had forgotten it was there.

But Ethel remembered, and now our project is to fix up the dollhouse and get it ready for our granddaughter Meghan, who is just at the age Ethel was when the dollhouse started its life more than half a century ago.

This dollhouse is a treasure to behold. It's about four feet all around. It has two full floors and a stairway between them, an attic, a front porch the whole width of the house, and a roof professionally shingled by roofer McCluskey. For easy access by little hands, he put two-story hinged doors on one side, a door to the attic in the roof, and even a paneled front door leading into the house from the porch. It even had wallpaper and inside light fixtures at one time, but they are gone now. It was certainly a beauty in its heyday.

Now we are carefully restoring it to give it new life—replacing some broken glass, window frames, and missing shingles; giving the porch new supports and a new roof; and painting it all over to make it a thing of beauty again, though we figure to leave to Meghan and her mom and dad and brother, Neal, the fun of interior redecoration.

Our daughter, Betsy—now quite grown up, of course—has pointed out that this has to be a family dollhouse. After Meghan has grown beyond playing with it, Betsy insists, the dollhouse must be reserved for the next girl in the family who's ready for it. And that's our plan.

We've been struck by how very fortunate we are to have a family heirloom like this old dollhouse released from basement bondage so that it can give new joy to another little girl.

In our modern mixing-bowl American society, it seems harder and harder to hold on to the old treasures we like to read about: family homesteads, china, silverware, furniture, toys, and the like. Houses don't seem to go from one generation to the next any more, the way they used to. Most families occupy a house for just one generation, and in the end homes have to be broken up, furniture is discarded, china and silverware are broken, and toys disappear. In the process, traditions are lost.

Ethel and I figure we have been given a rare opportunity to extend a family tradition—to send this little old handmade dollhouse on its way for another fifty years, or maybe more. Who knows how long, with proper care and love, this lovely dollhouse might go on, and on, and on?

—J.D.

WHEN YOUR WIFE'S IN THE HOSPITAL

When your wife has to go to the hospital for some serious surgery—I found out again recently—there's a fine moment when you realize that instead of plain all-out human worrying about her, you are much better off spending this terrible time of tension praying and asking God to help.

That awful chilling moment when your wife tells you about her first serious symptom sets off a frightening sequence of days and weeks of worrying. It helps a lot that we've been very close, through two wars, other operations she's had, six children being born and getting sick and having accidents, and now our getting older and becoming aware of all the things that can happen to us senior types.

That all helps one to know instantly the import of these threatening symptoms. And then you start your worrying.

You start with some basic unfocused worries—generalized all-purpose worrying about her well-being and your future life together. Worrying, though, like most human endeavors, seems easier to handle when you break it down into manageable parts. So pretty soon you go on to some specific worrying.

When she goes to the doctor that first time, you worry about what he'll find, although you have this terrible suspicion you know what it is. When he orders some preliminary outpatient surgery and x-rays and blood tests, you worry about what they will show.

And then, as in our case, when the preliminary surgery shows the need for some further radical surgery, you find lots more specifics to worry about.

You worry about how long she'll be unconscious during the operation, what sort of anesthesia she'll get, how long the operation will be, what awful things the surgeon will find, how long she'll have to be in the hospital. Is the doctor good enough, is he up to it, will the anesthesiologist do the job right, will she survive the surgery, and if so will they get the malignancy out, and if not will she live very long, will she die in the course of the operation, will she come out of it all right?

You go to bed at night worrying, wondering what the future holds for her, for you, for your children, your grandchildren. You wake up worrying about what challenges this new day will bring to you and her.

You'd be prepared to handle it all, you think, if you only knew what it might be. Deep down you are preparing for something awful to happen, and you are praying that you, and especially she, won't have to face it.

In a while also comes the realization that you've got to keep busy. There's work to be done at home—all those chores she did without your help you now have to try to do without much experience or finesse.

You have to get some clothes washed—and first find the supplies. You have to cook some food, and pretty soon you've become a student of Jeff Smith and you're the newest frugal gourmet in town. And then you've got to get the pots cleaned and the dishes and glasses washed, so you can do it all over again tomorrow. Having a wife in the hospital is good for a husband's education, humility, and psyche.

But soon, thank God, my experience shows, this period of just plain tense worrying and somewhat distracting busyness gives way to something much more meaningful—a period of talking regularly to God. This is also a very good time, I found out, to ask any saints with whom you identify or holy people you know, to help out and pray along with you.

We have a special group we call our "Holy Gang of Four" to whom I've learned to talk and pray whenever I think I have something they might want to hear.

Our holy gang is made up of our first baby, also named James, born on All Saints' Day, who died in his fifth month from sudden infant death syndrome; our niece, Sister Maureen, who died when she was just past thirty during a seemingly routine operation; Father Hugh Morley, a beloved Capuchin friend from Catholic Press days; and another dear editor friend, Father John Reedy, one of Notre Dame's Holy Cross congregation—all of them very close to my wife and me and our family.

I did my talking in the hospital chapel—stopping there each day on the way in to visit and on the way home, to tell them about our problem, our love, our hopes, and our dreams. They were good conversations, and we have been very fortunate, once again. Ethel's now back home in good health.

—J.D.

HAVING A BABY IS DIFFERENT TODAY

There's a difference these days, I've learned, in the way babies are being born—a lot of difference from the way things were when Ethel and I were a new mom and dad years ago.

There's nothing new about the way babies get started, I hasten to add, or about the way they come out into the world, and the resulting products look pretty much the way they always have—give or take some size or ethnic differences. But a lot of the other stuff about new babies—how they are prepared for and cared for—is different, I assure you.

When our sons and our daughter were born, many years ago, fathers pretty much stayed out of the way and out in the waiting room, if we stayed around the hospital at all. I remember that our several doctors uniformly advised me that there was nothing I could do, and I might as well go home. I usually did; I wasn't hung up on hanging around. So I'd go home and wait for the phone to ring.

Those fathers who did remain at the hospital were confined to the waiting room, where they walked and worried, sat and smoked, and talked with the other fathers-in-waiting. We were never, ever, allowed in the delivery room. It was just sort of understood that we would contaminate the labor room, the delivery room, the baby, the mother, and everyone and everything else really important in delivering that baby.

Somehow, however, in the intervening years, hospitals and doctors and nurses seem to have worked out the problems we fathers presented years ago. Fathers today are part of the action, all the way. Many of them go to courses with Mom before the baby comes, and many go into the hospital with their wives and *stay* there to help with the delivery itself. It's something to applaud!

Ethel and I have just returned from Colorado where we played with and cuddled a brand-new miracle, our third grandchild, Conor Daniel Doyle. Conor's mom and dad, Sharon and Peter, went together to natural-birth classes for months before he was due. They learned together about proper diet and exercise and other good things for the baby.

But Sharon never got to the part of the course that tells you how to breathe while you're having the baby. Conor was born seven weeks prematurely, weighing four pounds nine ounces, and she had to get along with on-the-job training for the rest of it.

Sharon started having contractions five minutes apart four days before the baby was born. Peter not only whisked her off to the hospital but stayed with her there for two nights. And I mean *stayed* there. He slept the first night on a cot right next to her bed, and then the next night they moved him to a gurney, one of those wheeled hospital beds. That would not have happened in my fatherhood days!

Then Peter went back to work, and somehow Sharon and the doctors conspired to hold off Conor's arrival for four days. That delay in itself helped strengthen a premature baby for his entrance into the world, the doctors say. And they gave him, via his mother, some steroids to help his lungs, because lungs develop last and are vital for the new baby, and critical for the premature.

Sharon phoned Peter from the delivery room herself the morning of the day the baby was born—something else new these days—and told him, "I'm going into labor. You better get right over here...but take your time." They say he did the twenty-minute trip in twelve.

Peter was right there throughout the delivery, holding

Sharon's hand, helping with her breathing, comforting her. In a real sense he was an assistant on the delivery team—something the fathers of our generation never were, would never have been permitted to be, and, for the most part, never wanted to be. That's what's changed.

Peter remembers at one point one of the nurses telling him to look down, and he saw this fuzzy head of hair appear, and then the rest of the baby's body sliding out. He remembers thinking, "Good heavens, a totally new human being, and he's my son!"

The latest dispatch from Colorado is a good one. Conor passed his original scheduled birthday last week. He's over seven pounds now, and he's lifting his head and turning to the other side. And now he's giving his mom and dad some playtime in between his naps and feedings. We thank God, and pray he continues doing well.

I admire these young mothers and fathers who share the chores of getting ready for having and caring for a baby. Of course, tension and trauma are part of what they share, but they also share in the great joy of the miracle they have created with God, as we did in our time. That hasn't changed.

Another thing that hasn't changed: young parents are still awed by what they have done, and maybe a bit unsure of themselves. When it was all over, and Conor came home, Sharon asked her doctor, hesitantly, "What do we do with him *now?*"

"Well," the doctor said, matter-of-factly, "feed him and water him, and he will grow." And now he's doing just that.

—J.D.

LETTER TO A NEW GRANDDAUGHTER

D ear Rachel,
    It was a thrill for us to meet you yesterday, and to welcome you into our world—this sometimes wicked but for the most part wonderful place in which we live.

You slept through most of our visit, of course, but your grandmother and I understand. The very young and the very old are allowed to do that. After all, you were only twenty-seven hours old. And we must admit that sometimes this world of ours does get a little noisy and hectic; it takes some getting used to.

I noticed that your eyelids fluttered from time to time and you peeked out to look me over once or twice. You'll learn how to do that eyelid-fluttering thing a little better later on, I understand; your grandmother assures me it will soon be second nature for you, a marvel for your dad and other guys to behold.

You certainly picked a beautiful time to be born, I must say. Spring swells and glows in the early flowers we see now, beginning to warm the air, promising the peace and sun of summer. And just this morning I discovered a new generation of bumblebees courting the purple crocuses in our garden, and the daffodils are getting ready to pop into golden bloom. Did you notice the daffodils your dad brought from your own garden at home, for you and your mom in the hospital? "The world is charged with the grandeur of God," Gerard Manley Hopkins wrote. I think he must have been thinking especially about spring.

This is the best part of the year, I think, in which to start your time in our world. Not only because it's spring, but also because it's Easter time, with its thrilling message of life and God's ever-renewing love.

There are a few things I wanted to give you some advice about when we were together, but you seemed a little too new and a little too sleepy to pay much attention, so I'm putting them down in this letter instead:

You're just starting out new in our world, but it won't be too many years before you'll be ready to take charge of the world yourself—you and the other new people of your generation, the ones we saw in your hospital nursery yesterday and the others we didn't see, throughout the rest of our country and the world.

We all hope and pray that you and your contemporaries will do a better job than we have with this world God has given us.

There's no reason you shouldn't do well, of course. You are very fortunate to have been born here in this country, in this time. You will have the best of food, the best of love and care, the greatest opportunities for education, achievement, and influence. No other babies in all of history have had the great chances for joy and success that your class of 1991 will have.

Let me be the first to tell you, dear granddaughter, that young women of your generation will be able to accomplish almost anything you can imagine. You can be great doctors serving humanity, powerful lawyers, writers, artists, builders, sisters, social workers, professors, athletes, congresswomen, senators, Supreme Court justices, or maybe even presidents, if you think you might be interested in that chancy job.

Just think of all the wonderful role models you already have: Mother Teresa, Dorothy Day, your mother and your grandmothers, and all the other women you will learn to admire.

Be sure you eat well, Rachel, so you can grow strong and have great energy. Do what your mom and dad tell you to do; learn as much as you can; cultivate a love of art, reading, and music; travel and see the world; keep a sense of humor; and dream all the dreams that stir you. It won't be very hard to accomplish all you wish to do.

And remember this: without women, our civilization will wither and blow away. Only you and your female peers can repopulate our world. Not all of you will opt for bearing children, we know, but some will, and must. You, as woman, can provide the healthy haven the coming generation needs, for the future of our world.

For now, your grandmother and I wish you health and happiness, a wonderful family life, success and cheerfulness in all you undertake, and many lovely springtimes to come, in the peace of the Lord.

Love,

Grandpa

—J.D.

THE SUDDEN, SILENT DEATH
OF FALCO BOONIN

L ittle Falco Boonin died quietly and suddenly one night a few weeks ago, in Boulder, Colorado. He was only five months old, hardly even started in life, certainly too young to be leaving it. My wife and I were visiting when we read about it in the Boulder newspaper, the *Daily Camera.*

Falco lived with his mother, Rachel, twenty-three, in different places in and around Boulder. A lot of the time, according to the *Camera* story, Falco lived zipped up inside his mother's jacket as she wandered the streets of the city, followed by a pack of Labrador retrievers she kept.

The *Daily Camera* story said Rachel was homeless and had several times refused offers of free shelter, but her mother, who lives in Boulder, said, "Rachel wasn't homeless. There were places she was staying and could have stayed. It's a lifestyle choice she was making."

The night Falco Boonin died, he and his mom were sleeping in a little wooden playhouse in a small city park. It was cold: 31 degrees, the police said. When she awoke at daybreak on March 10, Rachel said, Falco was not breathing.

The investigating police sergeant said, "The child was dressed in a full set of clothes, a coat, a ski suit and was sleeping next to his mother in a sleeping bag. There are no indications of neglect and absolutely no indication that there is a crime involved here...no indication that the death was related in any way to the lifestyle of the child or his parent." A later autopsy by the Boulder County coroner's office confirmed all that and ruled out injury and exposure to the cold as causes for Falco's death.

He just died, for reasons no one knows. Dr. John Meyer, the coroner, said his office had found no medical explanation. "There's no cause of death in the usual sense," he said. So Falco's death was listed as sudden infant death syndrome— "a diagnosis of exclusion," they called it, when all other causes of death are eliminated.

Falco Boonin was one of an estimated seven thousand little babies who will die this year, suddenly, unexpectedly, without any apparent reason, and for whom the cause of death will be given as sudden infant death syndrome. But all that means is that no one has yet figured out why these babies die so suddenly and quietly, usually without even crying out. And no one has a clue as to how to stop it.

Forty-nine years ago our first baby died, silently, suddenly, on a sunny April afternoon, sleeping outside in his carriage. Little Seamus was, like Falco Boonin, just five months old. Nobody could explain it then, and no one can explain it now. We agonized then, and we still ask ourselves why? what happened? how could we have prevented it? though we know now we couldn't have.

It used to be called crib death, and sometimes mothers were blamed and even charged with smothering their children. Fortunately, times have changed, and most of the time police and hospital staffs are now more knowledgeable and sophisticated about sudden infant death syndrome. Usually they recognize the situation and the symptoms—actually, the lack of other disease symptoms—as they did in Falco's case.

But, sad to say, there seems to have been no real progress in finding a cause or cure in these nearly fifty years. When our Seamus died, few people were working on the problem or knew much about it. Now, several organizations exist to collect data, encourage research, and offer support to stricken mothers, fathers, sisters, and brothers.

Some research is being done now, it's true, but nowhere near enough. There just aren't enough people interested or enough dollars being applied to the problem—in large part, I think, because this is a deadly disease that doesn't leave a visibly disabled victim—just a terrible silence, an emptiness in the hearts and souls of thousands of families. So we keep up our hopes and prayers that one day soon some cause will be found, leading to an end, finally, to this silent, sudden killer of our littlest children.

—J.D.

THE YEAR OF THE GIRLS

This would be the year of the girls, our daughter, Betsy, said with confidence. She was predicting that the three new Doyle grandchildren to be born in 1991 would all be of the female persuasion.

For some generations, firstborns in our branch of the Doyles have always been boys, and two of the three babies scheduled for '91 were to be firstborns. So I scoffed at Betsy's suggestion.

As it turned out, Betsy was right. All three new Doyle grandchildren are wonderful girls, and we are delighted and blessed. Rachel was born in March and Tara in May—and now the third little girl has arrived: Lily Marie, a marvelous miracle born in Portland, Oregon, to Brian and his wife, Mary, an artist and Oregon native. As M. Chevalier sang, thank heaven for little girls!

One reason the new girl is called Lily is this verse by William Blake, Brian's favorite poet:

> The modest Rose puts forth a thorn,
> The humble Sheep a threat'ning horn;
> While the Lilly White shall in love delight,
> Nor a thorn, nor a threat, stain her beauty bright.

So Lily she became, on a rainy Oregon afternoon in late October. She is also named Lily, they tell us, for her mother's grandmother Eulalia—who was called Lily by everyone in Mary's family.

Lily Marie is a beauty bright, all right, with dark hair and a calm and lovely countenance from which her dark eyes study this strange and busy world she has joined.

When we saw her in Oregon, she was eating and sleeping most of the time, but for several periods every day also surveying her parents and us and those other people fluttering around her, clearly getting ready to propound some profound proposition when the moment is ripe. We can only wait to see what she may have to say.

One of the new girls of 1991 is living with us now, with her mom and dad, for a little while, so they can save up some money to buy a house of their own sometime soon. Talking about it the other day, my wife and I realized that having her in our home now is a rare and special privilege, not a problem as some might suggest.

Little Tara has infused new bounce into our tired and creaky legs, and brought forth new smiles on our creased old faces as she turns her crinkly smiles on us. She brings us daily joy and a measure of rejuvenation. Day by day now we see her growing, changing, reaching, trying, crawling, grasping, becoming a real person—in ways, I think, we never saw in our own children because we were too close to them and always too busy caring for them.

With our new girl—thirty years after our own last child was born—we are able to stand aloof from the hard parental chores of feeding, diapering, bathing, dressing, and medicating. We close our bedroom door at night and leave her and her problems to her mom and dad; in the morning we open our door to a new day of joy with our new baby for whom others are responsible. It's an arrangement of the times we live in that works for us and them, and we can recommend it to others.

We saw our triumvirate of new female grandchildren at Christmas, when we all gathered in Oregon for a Doyle reunion at a big beach house on the Pacific Coast. Sixteen of us were there—including our senior grandchildren, Neal and

Meghan, now thirteen and eleven, who first taught us about grandparenting and the special kind of love that it receives and gives.

We happily renewed our family traditions and love and welcomed the new girls of 1991 into our family circle.

—J.D.

WATCHING THE GIRLS GROW

I took four rolls of photographs of pretty girls last weekend. I felt like one of those fashion photographers you read about—shooting a hundred pictures from ground level, from above, and at different goofy angles, in the hope of getting a few really good ones for posterity and the photo album.

I was taking pictures of two of my pretty granddaughters—one three and one going on three—who were at our house for one of their rare visits together. They live thousands of miles apart—one here in New York and one in Oregon, and they don't often get to see each other or play together.

The young lady from Oregon was back East with her mom and dad for another reason, and they stopped by in New York on their way back home. So these two little girls were able to spend a couple of precious days together, with my wife and me and their mothers and fathers in attendance. It was a golden and fascinating opportunity to watch the girls grow, to be a quiet witness as these young cousins begin to get to know each other better, starting what we hope will be a close lifelong relationship between themselves and the third little granddaughter of about the same age who lives in Colorado and who couldn't join the party this past weekend. These three girls were all born in what I call "The Year of the Girls."

No longer infants, no longer just toddlers learning to get around, they are real little people, learning the processes and techniques of living, experiencing the wonders of the world, learning to connect with other people, finding out about playing together, loving, and sharing with others.

These three-year-olds we watched and photographed have already developed an enormous number of skills. They can talk and run and turn and stop suddenly and jump and hide and find Daddy when he's hiding. They can help fill a little pool in the backyard with the hose and then leap in and out of the pool again and again with glee and spray themselves and sometimes Mom and Dad as well. They can pour water in their hair and in the garden and laugh a lot doing it and rush off screaming for a towel.

They can eat a lot or not much at all and keep on growing anyway, and get very thirsty and drink from a glass like an adult, and sometimes spill a little and maybe even try to help clean it up. They can sit and enjoy having a book read to them, and want the same book read again and again, and they can maybe even read some of those letters from the book themselves, and carefully make a few, and draw some great and colorful pictures, too.

They can laugh and flirt a little with Grandpa, and cry sometimes because they're hurt or frustrated, and they can recover quickly without remembering the hurt or the anger. They can give, and receive, great joy and happiness.

Not long ago we went off to Chicago to watch our oldest granddaughter graduate from elementary school, and we're looking forward to being on hand when she and our other grandchildren reach their next milestones in life—graduations, birthdays, whatever.

With many others in our generation, we've been given the great gift of seeing our grandchildren come into the world and then watching them grow and blossom into wonderful new people, great new citizens of society.

Sometimes it's fun just to sit and dream about the relationship these three little girls and our other grandchildren will have in their future years. Will they continue to be close to one another throughout their lives? Might they go to the same colleges or universities? What careers will they choose: Church, government, foreign service, communications, military, business, sports? What great things will they accomplish? Who and where are the people in whom they might get interested, maybe marry?

Idle speculation, maybe, but great fun for Grandfather and Grandmother watching their granddaughters play on a sunny summer day.

—J.D.

Waiting for the Twins

In Oregon, in the chill, rainy days of the turn from October to November, we waited for twin grandchildren to be born, the first twins ever on the Doyle/Clancey side and, to our knowledge, the first twins in their mother's family as well.

With today's marvelous medical equipment and knowledge, we all had known for many months that there were twins growing and moving in their mother's uterus, getting bigger, stronger, preparing to arrive in our strange, wonderful, painful, frightening, beautiful world.

The ultrasound technician showed us pictures of the babies, pointing out a head here, an arm there, lips and noses, even ribs. We had to take a lot of that on faith, of course. To us the images looked ghostly, vague, amorphous, like a scene from a science-fiction movie.

The doctors said they even knew the sexes of the twins and asked if Mom and Dad would like to know. They said no; they would be content to be surprised when they were born.

We couldn't really see the twins moving, but you could feel them shifting if you put your hand on their mommy's tummy. We could see their heartbeats, though, traced in patterns on the monitor, going steadily on, then spiking a bit when they were somehow stimulated. The nurse gave their mother a sweet drink once to show us how quickly they'd react, and their little heartbeats jumped up right away.

But along with all the good things the doctors and technicians could tell about the twins before they were born, there was also a bad thing: one of them had an incomplete heart—

only one ventricle instead of two—and would probably need surgery right away to help her or him survive.

So the days right after our arrival in Oregon were tense and ominous. We all—especially their mom—were torn between eagerness to have the pregnancy over and the births accomplished and dread of what might happen to that little baby with the faulty heart.

It was a dark and rainy, windy night when the twins were ready to be born. Mary's water broke around midnight, and she and Brian went off into the dark while we stayed home with their three-year-old daughter, Lily.

A dozen hours later, twin boys were born. The doctors wanted Mary to deliver naturally, and a lot of painful, exhausting labor ensued, but finally a Cesarean section was needed because the twins, competitive at the very start of life, were trying to push each other aside to emerge.

The boys are named Joseph James and Liam Robert, and it is little Liam who has the heart problem. They were both good-sized at birth—both over six pounds, and Liam even a bit bigger than his brother. Now, weeks later, both have regained some of the weight babies lose right after birth.

The very good news about little Liam is that so far he seems to be handling his heart deficiency pretty well. The surgical team was standing by when he was born, ready to do surgery if he needed it right then, but he surprised everybody by doing very well for the first few hours, then for the first few days, and then for the first few weeks.

Now the prognosis, they tell us, is that Liam probably won't need surgery for a couple of months. His faulty heart seems to be adapting to his life right now: he's eating well, sleeping well, and growing, along with brother, Joe.

So, suddenly, our grandchildren group has increased by $33\frac{1}{3}$ percent, from six to eight. We were privileged, we know, to be there for the big event. We were able to do a lot for

Mary and Brian and Lily and the boys when we were in Oregon—cooking, cleaning, laundering, putting Lily to bed and getting her up and dressed, gardening, fixing things around their new house—good stuff that grandparents can do, if they are fortunate and agile enough, to be of real help to kids and grandkids.

Now, back home, there's not much we can do to be of direct help. We keep in touch with the newly expanded family back in Oregon, supporting them from afar. And we keep in touch with God, too, praying for all of them and especially for little Liam with his fragile heart.

—J.D.

THE MAGIC OF A NAME

We have recently passed again through the prescribed period of grandchild anticipation, not knowing if this ninth grandperson would be a boy or a girl (because the child's parents didn't want to be told ahead of time) and therefore, it follows, not knowing what the name of this new member of God's family and ours would be.

We were clued in, toward the end, that if it were a boy, he would emerge as James, and if a girl, she would make her appearance as Colleen. Colleen Mary arrived a few weeks ago, tipping our grandchild scales in favor of the girls. The score is five to four—an imbalance our daughter calls the proper restoration of the natural majority. But she is prejudiced, having had to grow up with four brothers.

The new Colleen is a lovely little baby, not crying too much, but still keeping her mom and dad up too much at night. And she's clearly a joy for her older sister, Tara, who is almost four and has been waiting eagerly and patiently so long for Colleen's arrival.

This birthing and deciding on a name set us to thinking about names—the personal names we are given at birth and for the most part carry along with us throughout our lives.

You can change your name later on if you want to, but for most of us the names we were given at birth, through no choice of our own, stick with us and become as much a part of us as our hair, our eyes, our smiles, our persona.

When we first enter the world, our names are simply monikers our parents liked for some reason we may or may not know about, and they may seem strange and ring wrong in

the ears of our relatives. But as we develop our own personality and character our names begin to fit us, becoming real
and true and as special as we are. Repeated millions of times
by family and friends, a name worn well through life becomes unique and wonderful. "Who hath not owned," wrote
Thomas Campbell, "the magic of a name?"

Some names go on and on, repeating in generation after
generation, many of them biblical, solid, and reliable. And
some names seem to fade away in popularity, disappearing
from current naming lists. Some names are so popular they
become fads, almost irritating by their commonness.

Our generation of the family has several names that have
not been repeated in the names of our children or their children and will not likely be seen again among us—*Ethel,* my
wife's name, for example, and *Elmer,* my brother's name, and
Bessie, the name of my wife's aunt.

But *Bessie* is a variation of *Elizabeth,* one of the grand old
names in our tradition that happened to come out *Betsy* for
our daughter. And the names of our sons—*John* and *Kevin,*
Brian and *James, Peter* and *Joseph,* and *Thomas* and
Patrick—I think, will always be around in good repute.

In our gang of grandchildren we have some great old names
as well—*Rachel* and *Daniel* and *Joseph* and *Mary* and *Robert*—along with some lovely new ones, like *Lily* and *Marie.*
The names of our grandchildren also lean heavily to the Irish.
We now count one each *Neal, Meghan, Conor, Tara, Liam,*
and *Colleen*—six out of the total nine. German, the other
part of our heritage, fares not very well, I'm afraid.

When we told her the new baby's name, an Irish friend of
ours remarked, "Colleen? That's not a name; that's a descrip-
tion." We laughed politely, but we disagree emphatically. It's
a real name, and it's unique, as she is—the dark-haired Colleen lately welcomed to our family circle.

—J.D.

OUR YOUNGEST CHILD MARRIES

Our youngest son, Tom, was married last week. After months of preparation, and the excitement of the wedding week itself, he and Diane are happily embarked on their new life together.

They are also embarked on a honeymoon that seems extraordinary to my wife and me and that we see as a sign of the changed times in which we live: they flew off to a little island called Saba, the top of an extinct volcano in the Dutch Windward Islands, for a scuba-diving honeymoon.

Joyful as we are at this latest nuptial event, we also recognize that this wedding of the last of our boys is a highly significant milestone—one of the last markers on the road my wife and I took at our wedding years ago.

The generation of children we begot has now fully matured and started down new forks in the Doyle road. Now Tom and Diane's newest branch of the family road will gradually widen, helping to carry along the family traditions and name.

A wedding is a cosmic event—a time when one's family experiences instant expansion, welcoming a new adult member in a wonderful sort of explosion. It wasn't very long ago that my wife and I had a family of four boys and one girl. We have now turned into a family of five daughters and four sons, plus our grandsons and granddaughters.

Weddings give fathers and mothers a rare opportunity to take in, instantaneously, new daughters and sons, without the pains and pressures of bringing them up, without the daily family dramas. We welcome them into our families at the best of times—when they are young but mature, filled with promise and potential, sparkling with love and hope.

We can tell these new family members about our family and its milestones, and we learn from them about their families, their roots and backgrounds, their growing and maturing, their successes and failures, their hopes and dreams.

My wife and I figure that anyone who has come to love one of our children enough to marry him has to be very special and perceptive, and by that fact alone qualifies for our lasting admiration and affection.

A wedding—at least at our house this week—also teaches everyone valuable lessons about patience, sharing, forbearance, courtesy, humor, togetherness, and love.

All of our family stayed with us. For several days before this wedding, and several days after, our small house was crowded, disarranged, noisy, and happy. Somehow, living on top of one another for these days helped to cement our family ties.

It was important to all the boys and all their wives—our daughter-in-law Mary pointed out—for everyone to stay in the house for a family event like this, and not go off to stay in a more comfortable motel or with friends. In the house the boys can return to their youth, remembering the good and bad times of their childhood, repairing any hurts they may have inflicted on one another, reinforcing their sense of coming from the same source, and preparing to carry on the family traditions.

For their part, the wives of our boys like to stay in the old house because it brings them closer to their husbands' origins. Living in this expanded family atmosphere, even for a brief time, makes them new partners in the family's past and future. And the grandchildren soak up family stories, laughter, and love, beginning to understand what their fathers, mothers, grandparents, uncles, and aunts are really all about.

So this past week, this old house, where often before we had trouble fitting in ourselves and our five children, somehow housed thirteen Doyles in confusion and harmony.

There were Doyle men, wives, and grandchildren in two bedrooms on the first floor, in a makeshift bedroom downstairs, and even upstairs in our finished attic. They slept surrounded by furniture not yet taken away to new homes, by boxes of books and record albums and games and old school papers and other mementos of the years of growing up.

Now they have returned to their own homes and places of work, but we know that by this wedding we have all been mightily reinforced in what our family means to us; we are better family people, more in love with one another and more welded to our family than ever before.

—J.D.

THINGS WE NEVER TAUGHT
OUR CHILDREN

I was having this nice conversation the other day with Tara, our four-year-old granddaughter. She and her mom and dad and baby sister had gone up to visit our daughter in Dutchess County, and Tara was telling us all about it on their return.

Her account of what they saw, the places they went, the motel they stayed in overnight, the meals they ate in the diner, and the fun they all had was cogent, animated, and very well spoken.

A question suddenly occurred to me: how and when did she learn to speak our language so well? After all, she's just a little kid, not even in school yet. How did it happen that already she can carry on such articulate conversations, only rarely using an incorrect word or phrase or pronouncing something a little off base? How do children all over the world, in fact, learn their languages so quickly and use them so easily?

The answer, of course, is something like osmosis. Kids soak up words, sounds and syllables, thoughts, pictures, and concepts minute by minute, hour by hour, day by day. They repeat what they hear—first one word at a time, then in groups of words, and later in sentences. Somehow language—complete and correct in usage and vocabulary—passes into a child's brain, and from there it's sent to the voice box and tongue. Surely the human capacity for language is one of God's miraculous inventions.

And if Tara and billions of other children learn to speak a complex language without anybody's really teaching it to them, the question arises, what other things have our children learned that we never taught them?

Some things, yes, we actually teach kids—arithmetic, writing, and riding a bike, with some adult flying after them, trying to prevent a crash. Tying shoelaces, brushing teeth, fastening buttons, and zipping zippers—all these have to be taught, sometimes slowly and tediously. "Those that do teach young babes," Shakespeare wrote, "do it with gentle means and easy tasks."

Children must be taught to use a knife and fork and spoon, and to say the magic words *please* and *thank you* and *excuse me,* and not to use some other not-so-magic words, which I'll not specify, which sometimes they also absorb and spring on you anyway. And we teach them that reading, music, art, dance, sports, and all the rest are good things to do and enjoy.

But there are lots of other things we never teach our children that they learn anyway. I don't ever recall teaching our sons, or our daughter either for that matter, how to use a screwdriver, or a saw, or even a hammer. But I do remember many Saturday afternoons when I stood tinkering at the workbench downstairs, listening to Notre Dame football games on the radio, and they would happen by and wonder what I was doing, and I would try to explain. They picked it all up, somehow, as part of their education by osmosis.

We teach our children, and our grandchildren too, in ways we're not aware of. By means of our actions and words, they learn from our example: that honesty is best, that cruelty to others in word or deed is a very bad thing, that abuse—physical or verbal—is wrong, that loyalty and friendship and fairness and justice are good and cynicism and cheating are not. And they learn to believe in God, to love one another, and to pass their faith on to others.

One time Brian, maybe ten at the time, came home to tell us he was marching in the May procession at school, but he was disgusted, he said, because he had to march with Emily. You know the way they used to process at Catholic school, and maybe still do some places: girl and boy side by side, eyes downcast, hands together, under Sister's stern gaze.

We knew Emily to be a pleasant and bright girl he should have been happy to walk with, but we also knew she was one of the few black children in our school. We were horrified at the thought that we had failed our son in this basic lesson of equality and love of all God's people.

Very carefully, barely breathing, we asked his reason. He seemed surprised by our question, especially since he knew we knew Emily. "Why, you know," he said, to our huge relief. "She's a lot taller than I am!" That was all that really bothered him about Emily.

—J.D.

Doing Your Grandparent Thing

I think being a grandparent is a more active, more energetic, and more demanding job than it used to be. It's not enough these days to *be* a good grandparent—not enough just to be there at home when your grandchildren come to call or phone; not enough just to wait and watch for the mailperson to bring you those beautiful, scrawled child's notes from across town or across the country.

You and your spouse started it all, remember, and now, years later, you aren't quite finished yet. You have a further obligation of your parenthood—to stay active in this new role, to do your grandparent thing properly, working hard to make sure your grandchildren get to know you well.

They need to learn what you look like, get to know the smell of you, know how you laugh and how your arms feel when you hug them, how much you love them, how much they mean to you. They need to store the things you tell them deep in their memories, for recalling later when you are gone.

As we have welcomed our own grandchildren and visited them in different places over the years, my wife and I have developed a seven-point plan of action for keeping in touch with them—for doing our grandparent thing:

1. Go frequently to see your grandchildren in their native habitat, even if they live far away and even if it costs more than you think you can afford. Cut some corners and find the money. Stay with them a day or so. You need to be part of their daily lives from time to time— several times a year if you can manage it.

Do your visiting while they are young, before they get too much involved in other activities and too old for grandparenting things—and while you and your health, energy, and money hold out.

2. Share family facts and legends with them. Tell them stories, sing them songs, show them photos and artifacts from your children's childhood. Tell them about your own youth—the Depression, the war, your first job, your parents and grandparents, the places you and your family have lived.

   You might want to create a family tree, as our oldest son, Kevin, has done on his computer. He keeps adding to it as he gets additional information from family members, and now it has become a vital source of family knowledge for all of us and for generations to come.

3. Put together photo albums and present them to each of your grandchildren—and your children, too, for that matter. Go through all those photos you've taken over the years, organize them in albums, and give each of your children and grandchildren her or his own album in which each one is the star of the show.

4. Invite your grandchildren to come and stay with you, when they are old enough. But have them come separately and singly, to avoid competition, friction, and stress on you. Have them stay a week or so, during the summer or a school vacation, and make each an honored guest.

5. Send them mail often; everybody likes getting mail. Brief letters, postcards, little thoughtful gifts show you are thinking of them. Pretty soon you'll find them doing the same—sending you little notes and drawings and mementos.

6. Share with them your own life philosophy. Tell them the things you think are important in life—faith, education, generosity, concern for others and the environment. Be

sure to tell them some of your family joys and family tragedies, and let them know how important God is in your life, and how God has helped you and your family along the way.

7. And be aware of some cautions: Don't be demanding or overbearing as a grandparent. Don't smother your grand-children, or get in the way of your own children's pri-vacy. Give them all room, but give them love.

It's a tough job doing your grandparent thing, isn't it? You just have to keep working at it.

—J.D.

Our Adult Friends: Our Kids

We have these five adult friends we see from time to time. Nice people, friendly, good family background. They look a lot like us and talk somewhat like us, and their mannerisms are similar to ours. And we have a special interest in them because they are our children.

These special friends of ours are all now well past the age we were when we begat them, and it has dawned on us now that we must no longer think of them as our children but as our early-middle-aged friends (how they will hate to hear that) who happen to be related to us.

They have their own offspring now, most of them, and their children outnumber them almost twice over. Their nine new kids in our exploded family unit range from seventeen years down to seventeen months. They seem much easier for us to handle than our own progeny were. It turns out that having grandchildren is a lot simpler than having children used to be.

Our own kids—the models we brought out back in the '40s, '50s, and '60s—are now too old to be children, anyway. They don't even look like children anymore, and haven't for a long time. Some are bearded or mustached, running a little to fat. Some wear glasses, have aches and pains already, and are showing some gray in their hair.

We count them still as our beloved children, sure, but now more as dear friends who came from my sperm and my wife's egg and grew up in our house and ate from our table and gave us lots of headaches and copious joy. And then took off for various other parts of the country.

Thinking of our children as close adult friends allows us

to make that very desirable move—away from them and their day-to-day affairs. It allows us to lead our own lives our way and allows them to raise their own children, make their own homes, and live their lives minus our constant attention and participation.

It's a liberating experience for them and for us, confirming what we already know but sometimes hesitate to admit— that they can indeed function in society and in the world without us, as they will have to do after we die. It's not too early for them and us to get used to that idea.

When they come to visit us, we welcome them as dear friends who have returned to relive their younger days. They laugh a lot and sprawl on the couch and the floor, making the house seem more crowded that it ever was before, because now they are so big. They run around heavy-footed and wrestle and jostle one another raucously. They shake the house with the joy that bubbles up naturally from old friends coming together and remembering their days as kids. It's a pure pleasure to behold.

We provide for them as we would for other old friends, offering food and drink, beds to sleep in, old family movies to hoot at, late-night rambling conversations, and lots of love and freedom to do as they wish. We treat them with courtesy and respect and concern for their privacy and feelings. We give advice when it is asked for but not otherwise, and we try not to be resentful if they don't take it. They have a right to ignore our suggestions but not, of course, to ignore us. In the end, we bid them all adieu and return to our quiet lives.

Spouses of our related friends, we think, should be treated with special care. They don't carry the baggage of being our children—which can be a very heavy burden indeed—but they do have that special distinction of having been chosen by our kids, who selected them from all the rest of the world to be married to.

But because of and at the same time in spite of that special status and distinction, they will always be a little nervous, wondering how we view them, and if we love them half as much. As the progenitors, we have an obligation to show them regularly that we really do.

When, sometimes, we go to visit these dear adult friends of ours, we too try to act like good old friends just visiting them, not as Matriarch and Patriarch on an inspection tour. It's another part of our respecting their lives and their respecting ours.

Then, the next time they come home to visit us, we say once more, "You're very welcome, old friends. It's nice to have you back!"

—J.D.

PART 2

A HOME IN THE WORLD

B irth, schooling, puberty, a thrashing into maturity, and then, for the rest of our lives, the yearning for communal love: the great human itch is to belong to a family of any sort, all sorts—familial by blood, neighborhood, avocation, occupation, religion, politics, gender, whatever will bind us to others and hold us all in a strong net. We search for community almost desperately, in fanciful childhood memories and golden pasts that never were quite so glittering, in jittery moves from town to town. We want to be home. Here are essays about that curious and powerful place.

Our Unique Generation

Those of us who were in our late teens or twenties in World War II, then "thirty-something" during the Korean War, and who are today's much talked about senior citizens, are part of a unique generation—quite different, I think, from our parents' generation and from the generation of our children.

Ours was the first, and maybe the last, completely child-oriented generation. We and our contemporaries produced the baby boom. In the process of establishing homes, raising our children, building our careers, and now entering our senior years, we have changed the face and form of the world.

In our child-producing years, having three or four children was typical, having five or more not unusual. Even a couple with eight or ten children was not considered gross, as might be the case today: they were just thought to be a bit more Catholic than the rest of us.

Most of the men who went off to World War II were just kids themselves when they left. But they were seasoned world travelers, mature adults, when they returned. They were away three, four, or more years and went through the greatest experience of their lives, one that, for most of them, nothing else would ever rival.

Back home, their wives or girlfriends suffered years of loneliness and worry, never knowing just where their men were, whether they would ever return, or if they did, whether they would be maimed for life. Despite the worry and the waiting—or perhaps because of it— these young girls became mature, self-reliant women, quite able and ready for homemaking and child-rearing as soon as the war ended.

Women of our generation, with rare exceptions, were not career women. The majority stayed home with their children and put off any career ambitions; only when their children were grown did many of them seek jobs again. For most of them this amounted to giving up potential careers as teachers, doctors, politicians, or whatever else they might have been. It was a huge act of generosity and selflessness on the part of a whole generation of women, an act that has never been quite understood or appreciated.

Sociologists have rightly described the movement of our generation from the cities and towns of America to the newly burgeoning suburbs as a monumental national upheaval, which has led to the explosive growth of a non-city America living mostly in modest homes in a changing countryside sprinkled with shopping malls and supermarkets and paved with superhighways and parking lots.

This movement was another manifestation of our child-oriented generation at work.

We World War II people just wanted a little house with a garden and a place for the kids to grow up happily and peacefully. Why else would fathers have endured the long commutes that became part of our lives? Why else would the wives and mothers of these children have endured their lonely days at home with no one to talk to but the kids or other mothers wheeling their kids around?

Why did our generation have such dreams, make such decisions, and accept such sacrifices?

We who were lucky enough to survive World War II were optimists, ready and eager to remake the world. We were convinced that our victory assured us and our children, and their children, of a just and peaceful world in which to live.

For twenty years or so we seemed to be right. Our world of the late '40s and '50s did turn out to be a pretty nice place to live in. Our young, clever Catholic president even averted the grave danger of another world war, but then he and his people got us involved in the morass of Vietnam, and then he was killed, and somehow everything seems to have gone downhill from there. "Camelot," if it ever existed, is long gone.

And so our generation was formed in ways very different from those who were young in the years of the Vietnam War.

For our children and their generation, the tragedy of the Vietnam War experience was their watershed, the background for their passage to adulthood. They have grown accustomed, I am afraid, to government deceit, corporate greed, personal indulgence, and casual violence. Small wonder they are sometimes cynical and suspicious.

We grieve for them and their generation, and the future with which they must deal, while we count ourselves most fortunate to have been part of a simpler, happier, unique generation.

—J.D.

AMERICA'S NEW PUBLIC GARDENS

Going south to visit friends, my wife and I drove down Interstate 81 through Pennsylvania, Maryland, West Virginia, and Virginia, and along that scenic highway we were stunned by the beauty of the many wildflower plantings in the highway median and along the sides of the road.

For miles and miles, beds of cosmos, daisies, poppies, and other pretty annual blooms I could not identify as we sped by, brightened our eyes and cheered our hearts, reaching to the sun, waving in the winds, showing us their splendid pinks, blues, whites, and yellows.

Somehow surviving the pollution of the passing vehicle parade, they provide a wonderful screen of beauty, sometimes hiding traffic on the other side of the highway, sometimes just flowing like a river of color along the shoulder on our side of the road.

We were delighted to see this evidence of a growing concern for color and beauty, food for the soul, on the part of those in charge of highway landscaping. We've seen these marvelous displays of flower and shrub plantings in the East, Midwest, South, and way out West, and we presume they can be found pretty much everywhere in the country.

This is happening because back in Lyndon B. Johnson's administration, the president's wife, Lady Bird Johnson, made the beautification of America one of her pet projects, and we are the beneficiaries.

Mrs. Johnson inspired Congress to pass legislation funding highway plantings, and now a portion of federal highway funds distributed to the states is annually set aside for the beautification we noticed on our trip. Thank you very much, Lady Bird, and thank you, highway landscape engineers.

These wildflowers, shrubs, and flowering trees give beauty to the eye, peace to the mind, and a certain serenity to the souls of those in the stream of cars, buses, and trucks whooshing by. Just think how many millions of travelers' psyches these new public gardens are soothing every day. Thousands of accidents must be avoided, I would guess, because travelers are less stressed as they drive by, much relaxed by these plantings of beauty.

Not long ago, visiting in Illinois, we went to see an unusual new tourist site in the western suburbs of Chicago that was getting a lot of attention and publicity, and rightly so. On a multiacred tract of land, one of the local companies, AT&T, had turned the great lawn in front of its headquarters into a new sea of flowers, the area between the road and its office building sweeping away in waves of color. Whoever planned this display had designed it carefully and creatively, blending different plants and different colors in bands of beauty, turning the whole area into a lovely scene, a pleasure to behold.

And thank heavens it's not only on highways and by office buildings we see the installation of plant and flower beauty proceeding apace. Have you noticed the growing number of gas stations, restaurants, motels, and hotels that are installing displays of shrubs, wildflowers, and small flowering trees? And a word of thanks here for another great idea, the Adopt-a-Highway litter-control program, in which people from local clubs, companies, and communities help keep America's roads clean.

This is the time of year a lot of people take driving trips just to see the beautiful fall foliage in which America specializes. Leaves begin to turn red and yellow and shades thereof, painting hills and valleys with glowing colors in their autumn demonstration of nature's glory.

Our roads and highways are crowded with sightseers come to see the dramatic displays. One hopes they won't overlook America's new public gardens along the roads as they go.

"God Almighty first planted a garden," Francis Bacon wrote, "and indeed it is the purest of pleasures." It's a joy that we who occupy God's world are trying to help out.

—J.D.

MAKING FRIENDS FOR A
COUPLE OF HOURS

The other day I played golf with my friends John and Ray and Kim, and a few days before that I played with my friends Bill and Dominic and Jerry, and last week I played with my friends Rhoda and Betty and Frank.

Strangely enough, these were friends I had never met before and never expect to see again.

Each time I was just one of a group of individual golfers who happened to arrive, at about the same time, at the little nine-hole public golf course near my home where I usually play. Each of us signed up separately, as single golfers; then the starter put us together and sent us on our way as a foursome for the afternoon.

In the few hours we stayed together and played together—hacking away at the little golf ball, chopping at the fairway and sand traps, wandering off into the woods nearby—we became pretty well acquainted. We were friends, of a sort, for a little time.

Golf—especially public golf—is like that. It's unique as a sport, I think, in the way it brings together diverse and unacquainted individuals, quite by chance, casting them as close companions for a compressed moment in history, and at the end of that time sending them off on their separate ways, probably never to meet again.

It's a sort of microcosm of life itself: an experience of meeting new people—friends you just haven't met before, as the saying goes—learning to know one another, getting closer and closer, sharing some successes and failures, and parting at the end.

At first, we new friends are a little aloof and tense with one another, but that's partly because we come together on the first tee, which is in itself a strange and daunting experience.

On that first tee you have to stand out in the open, alone, bend over, stick a little tee in the ground, and balance your ball on it, as gracefully as you can. Then with only a few practice swings as warmup you try to be cool and coordinated enough to hit a good drive—all while a dozen other golfers in other foursomes stand behind you, waiting their turns to tee off, watching your sorry efforts to get started.

But after we get that first hole behind us, and as the holes progress, we new friends begin to relax and talk with one another. A few well-placed and well-timed questions—about families, backgrounds, or work—usually open up the gates of conversation and friendship.

I have lately talked with a recent retiree about his forthcoming move to Florida, congratulated another on his promotion and raise, rejoiced with a happy lady golfer on the birth of her new granddaughter, and shared the delight of another man just back on the course after bypass surgery.

We try to encourage one another: "Good shot, Eddie! Bad break, Len! The wind really took that one!" We joke; we tell a few golf stories—which we have all heard before—and in the way of golfers everywhere we lie a little about our golfing prowess, or lack of it, and about why we aren't doing very well that day.

Equipment, wind, and weather are blamed a lot: old clubs, or new clubs, or slippery grips, or grips too rough, or old shoes, or new shoes too tight, or the wet fairway, or the dry greens, or the wind, or the sun, or the dark clouds.

There is one inexorable limit to the bounds of our friendships, however. Public-golf-course players who are put into foursomes together never give their last names. They introduce themselves on the first tee by first names only. "I'm Jim," I say, and they're simply Bob, Chuck, Sam, or Sally.

On the last green, as we retrieve our balls from the final hole, we say good-bye to these friends of a few hours. This ritual involves a handshake and a smile, then, "Enjoyed playing with you...nice round...hope to see you again soon." But you know you probably won't ever see any of them again.

For a brief moment, though, as our four lives intersected, we were four pretty good friends—four musketeers, sort of, tackling one of life's enjoyable little challenges together. And it left a warm spot in our hearts.

—J.D.

CLANCEY'S LAWS

My wife, whose family name is Clancey—always spelled with an *e*—has been promulgating certain rules for sensible eating and living for lots of years. Now the world is catching up to her. Compost is in, and worms, and potato skins, and organic vegetable growing, and lots of other good stuff. But we who have listened to Clancey's Laws all these years knew these things all along.

Of course, this current Clancey, my wife, is not really the originator of these rules. They come partly from the inherited folklore of the Clanceys and McCluskeys and Salmons. And, of course, the Irish have no corner on such wisdom, contrary to what the Irish themselves may think. Surely it comes in all manner of languages, multiplied many times over in cultures around the world. But Ethel has passed them on to us and made sure over the years that we have observed the laws, so she surely deserves some public tribute now that much of the world has adopted her wisdom in these matters.

For years, we've been putting into a gallon jar under our kitchen sink all the parings, coffee grounds, egg shells, and other food-preparation leftovers bound for the backyard compost pile. Neither I nor our children have been permitted, as long as anyone can remember, to just throw garbage like that in the trash. The good stuff—what can be dug in to make compost, new soil for the future—must be put in our special jar. It's one of Clancey's Laws: return to the earth part of what one takes out.

For years my sons and I have dutifully trudged out to the backyard to dig the day's compost into our little vegetable garden. Only on the coldest days and nights, when the earth's surface is frozen, have we been able to slip out of this digging-in obligation. But knowing how fast compost starts to break down, this is not an obligation one wants to overlook for very long.

Years before *The New York Times* discovered worms, and what they can do for compost, we were growing our own colony in the compost pile out behind the garage. And years ago our boys found our compost pile the perfect place to find bait for fishing.

One spring not long ago we noted a shoot, then the stalks and leaves of a mysterious plant we had not planted in our garden—something obviously growing from one of our compost digs. Would we get a pumpkin, cucumber, zucchini, or something exotic? Soon a blossom, then a fruit appeared, and grew and grew until we recognized, finally, one single acorn squash—grown from the compost we had dug in months before.

Clancey's Laws also taught us that you don't need insecticide on your roses—just soapy water from your sink dumped over the plants will protect them.

Red pepper sprinkled around your bulbs as they start to bud and flower will keep the squirrels away; but don't rake away the browning leaves of bulb plants because that weakens them for the next year.

You don't need to bother with the disinfectant sprays in your bathroom, either. Just burn a candle for a few minutes and the odors will be gone.

Never sit down without having a machine (the washer, dryer, or dishwasher) working for you. That's another of Clancey's Laws—a good and practical statement of the need for economy of time and proper utilization of energy.

Our Clancey rule-giver has always said we must let our water run five minutes before using it for cooking or making tea or coffee, and always draw cold water. Now we read that this is the correct and proper way to keep the lead and other chemicals that might be in the water out of our food. And wouldn't you know: we have just received a notice from our water company telling us to do what Clancey's Law has been telling us for years.

But there is one of Clancey's Laws I haven't yet subscribed to. She insists that avocados are delicious, nutritious, and one of God's great gifts, and she eats them all the time. I say avocados are dull and tasteless, and no, thank you very much. But otherwise I'm a believer in Clancey's Laws.

I recommend you turn to your own rule-giver for more of the same. Listening and paying attention as the wisdom flows will do it.

—J.D.

THE REBIRTH OF
OUR NEIGHBORHOOD

Our neighborhood is a pretty noisy place these days. That's partly because it's summertime, and the livin' is easier, and the noises of these warmer days and nights penetrate our homes more readily.

With our storm windows out, screens in, and doors sometimes standing open, we hear every growling lawn mower, whining leaf blower, or snapping lawn edger. We soak up the harsh sound of every car roaring into our dead-end street, and the strange joyless music of the current younger generation, wafting in from who knows where.

Children, suddenly a year older since last we heard them in the fall, now run screaming at their games in nearby yards. A Little Leaguer next door, all shining in his new Giants uniform, is off to do battle with the Dodgers—a living but unknowing commemoration of other good old days of New York baseball, now gone West.

On warm nights these weeks we know whose second-floor bedrooms are hot enough for air conditioners; by their hums you shall know them. We seem almost to be involved in the pool party we hear, somewhere a block or two away, as we too absorb the splashes and shrieks that go with whatever graduation, engagement, or birthday celebration is under way.

But there's another welcome reason our little neighborhood is not so quiet as it used to be.

Three houses on our block have been sold in recent months. For many weeks old rubbish has been thrown out and garage sales have been held. One moving van has taken one family's possessions away, and another has brought new family paraphernalia in.

New appliances have been delivered and their huge boxes put out and carted off. New lawn-service companies have been engaged and have already begun their loud ministrations. It seems for every advance in work-saving efficiency we must accept a new level of neighborhood noise.

The conversion of our neighborhood from old to new—the fulfillment of new ideas for these old houses—has begun. Construction work is progressing vigorously and noisily on several houses, as the new owners begin to modernize, modify, and expand their castles.

The changes are for the better, I am sure. Although they might surprise and disappoint the old owners, they certainly brighten up the neighborhood. Every new owner of an old house seems to have, as though it were some immutable rule, a different idea of how the house should look and what it should contain. That diversity is what makes home ownership so special.

I think if ever we sell our house, though, I'll plan not to come back and look at it again later. The new owners will probably make so many changes I'll be depressed either because they made it look so much better, or because they have changed forever the wonderful memories we had of the old, modest homestead.

In any case, the new owners are preparing the family shelters the way they want them. They are beginning the years of caring, feeding, educating, and developing their families in their private retreats, their homes—just as we and our former neighbors nurtured our children in these same houses, and watched them grow and, ultimately, go.

When we first moved here, it was because the schools we wanted for our children, and the church we attend, were only a few blocks away, and one could walk to the railroad to commute to the big city. In recent years we haven't had any commuters on our block, as people moved away or retired or took local jobs.

Our neighborhood is entering a new life now, having a rebirth. Neighborhoods don't stay the same, anymore than people do. Neighborhoods are born, have youthful years and middle years and older years, and then they enter new phases. They get new owners, new children, new hopes and dreams. It's part of the course of family growth and love.

—J.D.

A Neighbor It's Tough to Love

Everything that lives is holy, the poet William Blake wrote a couple of hundred years ago. But if old Will were still around, I would want to say to him, "Hey, Will, do you think that really applies to squirrels?" Personally, I have my doubts.

England has squirrels, I guess, and I imagine they were around when young Mr. Blake was writing, but he doesn't have a lot to say in his poetry about squirrels. "Tiger! Tiger! burning bright / In the forests of the night," sure, but not squirrels.

A lot of people can tolerate squirrels, and a lot of others never pay them much attention, and I suppose there are even some people who like them.

But some of us don't like them; can't stand them. Take my wife. She is an absolute pacifist—no war, no abortion, no capital punishment. She even captures spiders and those little water bugs with the round backs and carries them outside to safety. We are definitely a no-kill household.

Squirrels are another matter. Not that my wife or I would ever kill one, but she did buy me a slingshot when we were down in North Carolina so that I could take shots at the squirrels around here, especially after they have eaten her prized tulips. Fortunately for the squirrels, I haven't yet figured out how to sling shots at them without jeopardizing our neighbors and their children, windows, and cars.

It's not that the squirrels eat the tulip bloom itself, my wife tells me. They neatly nip the stem just below the bloom and eat the tasty stuff inside—the pistil—and leave the pretty petals strewn around the ground below. It's a vile thing they do.

The tulips are a foot off the ground, waving gracefully in the breeze, showing their beauty to the world. This means the squirrels have to stand on their hind legs or reach up and pull the stem down to do the dastardly deed—but somehow they do it several times each blooming season. We've never caught one in the act, actually, and it would be very hard to prove in a court of law that they did it, but there's no doubt about it in our house.

The editor of our Catholic newspaper has confided to me that she also has been victimized by squirrels. For three years running now squirrels have dug up and eaten her spring-flowering bulbs after she plants them in the fall.

In our neighborhood they don't dig up and eat the bulbs, but they dig little holes in our front yard, looking for acorns, and when they find some they leave the shells and scraps all around the lawn, like untidy picnic guests. They build their nests high up in the trees, messily chewing off the tips of branches for their nests and dropping the extra pieces to the ground. When they're in their nest-building mode, it seems to be raining little twigs and leaves.

Once we even had a careless squirrel come tumbling down our chimney, to our great surprise, and its own. It landed, terrified, behind a roaring fire we had blazing in the fireplace.

Quickly, we put out the fire and built a makeshift plywood cover over the fireplace opening. Then we rigged up a trap door and a garbage can baited with peanut butter. All night I sat silently by the fireplace, ready to slam the trapdoor shut when the squirrel might scamper out into the garbage can. But it never did.

The next morning, after I went to work, the squirrel gnawed through the wooden cover and ran into my son's room. Together they raced to the front door, and out the squirrel went as soon as it was opened.

Squirrels have no predators, at least not in our neighbor-hood. Dogs don't seem to care anymore, and cats around here are fat and lazy. Squirrels have the place pretty much to themselves.

I know we're supposed to love all God's creatures, but it's tough to love squirrels. I even have to wonder if Saint Francis of Assisi, who so delighted in God's works as revealed in nature, liked squirrels. Were there any squirrels living where he lived in Italy? Did he really know and love squirrels? Prob-ably.

I guess it takes a saint to be a lover of squirrels. I doubt we'll ever make it.

—J.D.

CLANCEY'S LAWS REVISITED

I've learned some great things from my wife over the years—Clancey's Laws, we call them—family wisdom we are passing on to our children and grandchildren and are happy to share with you.

Clancey's Laws, you may recall, say you should always run cold tap water several minutes before making your morning coffee or tea—gets rid of those bad chemicals lurking overnight, waiting to pollute your morning "cuppa."

And dig those vegetable and fruit peelings into your garden as compost so that the worms can start making new soil. If you don't have your own garden plot, be generous: pass them on to a relative or friend. It's a good idea, though, to ask first, and not just show up one day with a jar of compost at their front door.

Now, in a continuing effort to keep the world up to date, I can report on a few new Clancey's Laws.

One is about vinegar. We buy it by the gallon because you can use it for so many jobs around the house in addition to making salads. Like soaking rusted bolts and screws to loosen them. Or soothing children's insect bites and stings. Vinegar also cleans streaky windows, countertops, and stains on carpeting. Mixed with a little salt, it cleans copper-bottom pots. And it kills weeds and grass in sidewalk cracks.

And here's a law about cutting your grass. If you don't have a lawn, share this law with the friend to whom you gave your compost. When you cut your lawn, don't rake it after mowing. Just let the clippings lie where they fall. They're mostly water, anyway, so you can leave them, and they will water and feed your lawn by themselves. You avoid raking and plastic bagging, buying fertilizer, and wasting water.

Another Clancey's Law about gardening is that getting out and mowing and digging are excellent exercise, as good as or better than any exercise you might spend money on. *Cooking* magazine recently reported that you can burn up fifty-four calories in a ten-minute planting session. Another of Clancey's Laws upheld!

Clancey wisdom has always promoted broccoli as a dinner vegetable and a healthy nibbler. I've always maintained, however, that our loving God would not have made anything so poor-tasting be really good for you.

Turns out I was wrong. Some doctors in Baltimore now report that broccoli has a compound that blocks the growth of tumors in laboratory rats and that may do the same in humans. I'm not surprised to learn that the same compound also occurs in cauliflower and Brussels sprouts. But the really good news is that modern science has vindicated another of Clancey's Laws. If this keeps up, I may have to go all the way in following Clancey's Laws and start eating zucchini and avocados and drinking Celestial Seasons Red Zinger tea.

Finally, there's Clancey's Law of disappearing good products. We've noticed that as soon as we find a good, simple, economical food or household product we like to use, the manufacturer somehow hears about it and in a fit of corporate perversity takes it off the market.

Remember rennet powder? It was a simple, flavored powder that made an easy-to-do, good-for-you pudding. Gone, but not forgotten by us. And Thomas's protein bread—a tasty loaf with few calories and low fat content. Not in stores anymore. Dijon rye bread? Good product, with tasty thin slices. Don't make it anymore, the Pepperidge Farm Store lady told us.

There was another product we used to use, made from

soybeans, that helped stretch chopped meat for hamburgers or meat loaf. Disappeared. And remember those little jars of chipped beef that with a little cream sauce on toast made an inexpensive tasty family meal? Gone now, and too bad.

There's no advantage to the truth of this law, of course, but it seems that Clancey was right once again.

So now we're pretty much up to date on Clancey's Laws. But I'll keep my ears and eyes open and make notes so that I can bring any more to your attention another time. Posterity demands it, even if you don't.

—J.D.

FRIENDS FOR FIFTY YEARS

Our old friends Bob and Kay were up here a few weeks ago for our son Tom's wedding. They live in North Carolina, where they moved after retiring a few years ago. We see them only rarely now—visiting them at their place in the Blue Ridge Mountains, or here when they come back to New York for a special reason like this wedding—but our friendship endures.

Ethel and I and Kay and Bob have had this remarkable friendship for just about fifty years now—and it's hard for any of us to believe it's been that long—ever since we first got acquainted during our younger days at college.

As a couple of couples we became very close in the spring of 1943, just before Bob and I went into the Army. We had both joined the Army's Enlisted Reserve Corps; most of the young men in college in those World War II days joined such reserve units—in the Army, Navy, or Marines. The deal was supposed to be that you could finish your final semester of college before being called to active duty.

It didn't work out that way, actually, for Bob and me. That year was a difficult one in the progress of the war, we now know, and the Army needed more men in a hurry. Although our graduation was set for June, we were ordered to report early in March for processing and, soon thereafter, for basic training. Off we went to Camp Upton, out on Long Island.

In the few weeks before we reported, Bob and I and Ethel and Kay became friends forever. With no idea of how long we two men would be gone, or if we might ever come back, or maybe return injured in some way, the four of us dealt with the war opening up before us pretty much by ignoring it—and the world and college and classes as well.

We concentrated instead on just hanging around together—talking and playing bridge—hour after hour in the college lounge—Queens College out in Flushing. The lounge security guard told us we were not allowed to use cards there (it was a different world then), and he confiscated our bridge deck. So we fashioned a tiny, secret deck of cards out of paper and continued to play surreptitiously and steadily for weeks.

Seeing Kay and Bob again recently after a lapse of many months brought back a lot of those memories, and reminded me of how important such a lifelong friendship has been and is to all of us, and can be to any married couple.

The only time our relationship was interrupted was while Bob and I were away in the Army. After we returned, our four-person friendship resumed, and it has in fact grown stronger over the years.

We have been more like family than friends. Indeed, I think we have been closer than many family members ever are.

We have helped one another steer steadier courses across the oceans of married life. We have shared the joys and pains of births, family deaths, illnesses and accidents, job changes, vacations, house moves, and our kids' growing and going off to college and getting married.

Outside of the wedding festivities occasioning this recent visit, before Bob and Kay returned to North Carolina, we got together for one of our typical evenings. We talked a lot, ate and drank some, played lots of bridge, argued about politics and people, solved the world's problems, and matched one another—women against men—in quizzes and trivia games. Thereby we reinforced the mutual love so important to each of us.

One key feature of our friendship is that we all have real affection and respect for one another. In some couple-to-couple relationships, the women may get along fine, but the men may not; or the men may be soul buddies, and the women have nothing in common.

A true couple-to-couple friendship can be an enormously important part of a married couple's life. It helps to provide stability for your marriage, a ready-made aunt and uncle for your children, a non-family sounding board for your complaints and plans and hopes, and a lasting atmosphere of esteem and affection. I'm happy to see our married children building such friendships themselves.

It's not easy to fashion and maintain such a lasting friendship. You can't advertise, you can't sign a friendship contract—as I was told recently one modern young couple wanted to do. You have to keep alert for friends like this, recognize them when you find them, and work hard at keeping such a relationship alive—for fifty years, maybe, or even more. Who can tell?

—J.D.

LOST: DOYLE ISLAND

The other day my wife was cleaning our little old globe of the world—the kind that sits on a stand and whirls around and around when you spin it. The globe is from sometime way back in the '60s—ancient in globe years, I guess—about the same age as our thumb-worn World Book encyclopedia volumes. And both are battered from many years of vigorous family consultation.

So Ethel carefully washed the globe and wiped it all over, scraping at a couple of really dirty spots down in Argentina, trying to get out some stains in the Atlantic off West Africa. "Wouldn't it be great," she said, laughing, "if we could clean up the world we live in as easily as this?"

"It surely would," I said. God could easily do that, I guess, as in the old days of Sodom and Gomorrah. *Swish,* and the whole world would be made clean again—maybe wiped off completely. Do you wonder sometimes if God might like to pack in this whole planet and start all over again?

Our old globe has been heavily used and much abused, I'm afraid. There's one ugly pencil hole in the Windward Islands and a bold red line across the Pacific from the Kuriles to Baja, California, made not by any explorer but by some Doyle student's errant pen.

My wife loves maps and globes, and faraway places fascinate her. She's a whiz on *Jeopardy* geography questions. She thinks geography is a far more worthwhile subject for high school students than algebra or trigonometry, more important than Latin or chemistry.

Her geography passion has been transferred to our children, who have traveled all over the globe, as lots of young people do these days. They've been to see Alaska and Alberta, Ireland, Italy, Greece and Greenland, mountains, oceans, and the depths of the sea. And now they live in exotic places with strange-sounding names like Colorado, Oregon, Illinois, Ronkonkoma, and Wappingers Falls.

Our family interest in geography takes other forms as well: others may play Trivial Pursuit, but our favorite table game is one called Global Pursuit by National Geographic. It takes hours to play, and it's a lot of raucous fun.

We do geography games in the car on long trips, too, including one our oldest son, Kevin, invented. As you drive along you mark off on a list he printed the states shown on the sides of U-Haul trucks passing by. The goal is to get all fifty states and the District of Columbia checked off in a year.

We have a fascinating shower curtain in our bathroom with a large map of the world on it, which you can study while relaxing in privacy. It's a teaching tool, too: our little granddaughter Tara asked me the other day to show her where her cousins live and how far away Oregon, Colorado, and Illinois are. Our family love for the faraway places of the world is sliding down to our grandchildren as well.

We try to give our children and grandchildren a sense of how important it is to know and understand other places and other people in this world God gave us.

Yet despite our passion for geography, our family has encountered a real geographic stumper.

Our youngest son, Tom, a scuba diver, not long ago brought up a set of very old Navy charts from the wreck of a World War I cruiser located in the Atlantic off Long Island. He's framed some of the best-preserved chart fragments and given them to family and friends, and you can even see some of them on display at the *Intrepid* Sea-Air-Space Museum by the Hudson River.

The chart piece he gave us has very special meaning for our family, but it's a puzzle at the same time. The main feature is Doyle Island, clearly marked but thus far a place we cannot locate on any other map or gazetteer and certainly not on our little globe on the shelf.

Doyle Island is in a string of islands with other names you might think would help us find it. There's Balaklava Island and the Gordon Group and Hurst Island and Heard Island and Bell and Boyle Islands and the Christie Passage. But none of those has yet helped us locate Doyle Island.

Maybe some expert in geography can help. Does anybody out there know where Doyle Island is? We would really love to know.

—J.D.

ON EAGLE'S WINGS

Our senior grandson, Neal Andrew Doyle, achieved a family first recently. He became an Eagle Scout, the highest rank a Scout can achieve, and something nobody else in our Doyle-Clancey family grouping has ever done. His father and two other of our sons and I were all in Scouting, and we tried, but we never made it as high as Neal.

To become an Eagle Scout, he planned and directed the refurbishing of a famous local totem pole in a forest preserve in the community west of Chicago where he lives. He raised money from local merchants for the project and got sixteen volunteers together to repair, recarve, and repaint the totem pole. They even moved nearby structures to show it off better, and Neal prepared some literature on the history and significance of the pole.

He received congratulations from lots of people, of course, including his godmother—his mother's sister, Carol—and our middle son, Brian, his godfather, who often offers advice to guide his godson along life's bumpy road. Neal is fortunate to have good godparents who keep in touch.

That's not always the case these days. I think one of the sad little secrets of the Church in 1996 is that godparenting is not well understood or held in very high esteem. Too often today, godparents are invited to sign up for the job casually, with no real sense of what it's all supposed to mean to them and the child, with few plans for their godparenting future.

Finding good godparents for your child today is not easy. A couple seeking to have their child baptized in the Church may have a tough time finding a peer, friend, or relative qualified and consistent in the faith. And that's because so many young people have drifted away from the Church.

So, at baptism, sometimes compromises have to be made. Yes, godparents are found, and they stand by the child at baptism, and they repeat the words the priest gives them, but often they never again advert to their special relationship to the child, or act the part again. Even the baptizing priest, I think, sometimes has to compromise—accepting the godparents offered without much confidence in how, or if, they will carry out their roles. Lots of prayers are said that it will turn out all right.

In his Eagle Scout message to Neal, Brian wryly confessed he was the only member of his Scout troop on Long Island who was asked to leave for "lack of ambition and failure to pay dues promptly." Despite that rejection, he said, he holds the Boy Scouts in great esteem, for three reasons:

"One, any organization which asks of its members that they become thrifty, reverent, diligent et cetera is a good organization. Two, the Scouts evince an organizational respect and affection for the land and the million creatures that are our cousins," and any organization that does so "is an organization with humility and zest and dignity.

"Three, the Scouts evince a similar respect and affection for the tribal peoples of North America, who were residents of this incomparable land as much as 30,000 years ago. Those peoples were here first, and we atone for their murders and uprootings best by telling their tales and by striving to understand how and why they lived on this land, in these woods, among these creatures and waters."

Totem poles like Neal's "were of enormous significance in the lives of the people who made them. They were art objects of stunning beauty…religious totems of immense spiritual power…talismans of community, of tradition, of the enormous power of story in the lives of tribal people.

"I live in the Pacific Northwest," Brian continued, "where the Klickitat and Klamath and Siuslaw and Nestuccan and Tlingit peoples of the coastal forest carved their poles from red cedar and made of them standing poems to the animals they considered their protectors, their cousins and brothers and sisters, their fellow travelers through this circle of the world.

"A Siuslawan boy about Neal's age would have had a totem animal to which he was attached by unbreakable bonds, about which he dreamed, which he would hesitate to kill, which he would seek out for wisdom. And perhaps that boy would begin to carve a cedar pole and make of that effort a prayer, a meditation, a gesture of respect.

"That is what Neal has done, and it has made him an Eagle Scout. I pray that he may always see good and evil from afar, that he will always be filled with great respect and affection for the land and its people and creatures, that he will remember with love those who have preceded him, that he will know, always, the respect and love we have for this young man, who once was a small boy and is now at the edge of a long manhood."

—J.D.

THOUGHTS OF HOME

Some weeks ago I was wandering through the thick copse of birches in my yard, idly looking for birds' nests and mouse bones. Instead, I discovered a totem pole I had never seen before. It shocked me. It was fifteen feet high, black, and topped with a peculiar grinning face. It stood next to a birch tree. The birch shone white against a knot of glowering oaks behind it. The pole was dark, erect, sudden: the birch tree's negative twin.

My neighbor planted the totem pole, he told me later. He is a famous artist and a good one. In his home are angels, demons, bears, roses, nudes, moons, birds, lovers. He is a whimsical and pragmatic man. "There are too many things to paint," he tells me. "I stay up late painting and get up early to paint." He paints in his home, having learned over the years that there he is most comfortable, most himself.

"At home I am me," he says, smiling. "Away from home I am a famous artist."

Another story, also about home. My brother Peter is a cabinetmaker, a wonderful one. He carves poems with his hands. Years ago he also rebuilt his house, turning a small and ancient cottage into a spacious and comfortable home. He cut no corners and did the work himself. Even the lintels are beautifully carved and carefully shaped to their particular corners.

In his home he and his wife and son welcome visitors of every stripe, shape, and color—except one. There is a woman in Wyoming who may not enter his home. Once she was married to a dear friend of Peter's. The man came home one night to find his wife in bed with another man. The couple divorced. The man now lives quietly with his ancient dog, who walks backward in the mornings before he gets his bearings straight. His former wife lives in Wyoming with the other man.

The woman wants to visit Peter's home. "Live and learn," she says. "Forgive and forget."

My brother's wife agrees with this. She sees no point in dredging up the past. "Life's too short," she says, reasonably. "What happened happened. It's over now. We should all move on."

"I forgive," says Peter, "but I do not forget, and in my home there will be no breaking of promises, no cheating, no dishonesty. Therefore she may not enter this home. I wish her well, I hope she's happy, but I do not want to see her within these walls."

My brother is not cruel, or chauvinistic, or insensitive. Quite the reverse: his sensitivity is enormous, and he feels things deeply. The pain of others cuts him to the soul. But he is also a man of firm beliefs, and one of those beliefs is in honesty. Your word should mean something, he thinks, even if you regret having given it. I suspect that he regrets some of the promises he's made. But I can't remember a single time since we were crewcut boys mistaken for twins that he's lied or broken his promise.

Nor is Peter stupid. He knows the world lies. But he feels that his home is the only place where he can control dishonesty, forbid its presence as much as he can.

A third story, my father's. His family moved many times when he was a boy: Pennsylvania, Ohio, Indiana, New York. Since high school he has lived in New York. He went to college in New York. He married in New York, brought up his family in New York, has lived in the same New York house with my mother for forty-one years.

Yet when I once asked him where he felt at home, he said, "I have no home. I feel at home nowhere."

He didn't say this melodramatically; it was simply a statement of fact from another honest man. He has no home. He likes the family house; it's done well to hold the many lives hatched and grown within its walls. But it's a house to my father. Not a home.

I listen to stories of home, sifting for its essence. Everyone has a story and each is different. I ask about home, and people show me pictures of security, warmth, rootedness, peace, family. Sometimes they mean a memory of when they were loved. They talk of simmering onions and fresh-mown grass, of the bustle of brothers, of kitchens and attics and cousins, of neighbors shoveling walks unasked, of children hopping fences, small girls in wading pools, cookies and cocoa for the postman. "A home is where a child buries a goldfish in the backyard," says one friend. "No," says another, "it is where you take refuge, it is where you take your shoes off and sigh in relief and have a favorite chair molded to your shape."

On the night the Persian Gulf War erupted, my wife, sobbing uncontrollably, told me she wanted to go home to Oregon. She hadn't lived in Oregon for seven years, but Oregon was home. To her, the memory is redolent of independence and dependence in the proper proportions. I strive to hear what she's really saying when she says home. She tries to show me, using her hands. I think what she holds in her hands is peace, which runs through her fingers like water in a place far from home.

Half a lifetime ago I left the home in which I grew up. My parents still live there among their books and memories and the papery voices of the children who are gone. Since then, home for me has been fleeting. Once it was an island where I came ashore after a long time at sea. Once it was a house where the sea licked the lawn and ducks slept on the porch.

Now, again, for a moment I know will pass, I am at home in the ancient house in which I live with my wife. We don't own it. We don't even rent it; we're caretakers. But I feel at home here for reasons I grope to understand. The feeling has something to do with the land of stories on which the house stands, with the dense, brooding thicket of birches and brambles that rings it. Built in 1840, the house has held many people in its hands: a doctor, a judge, a historian, a schoolmaster, a poet. A hundred children have thundered through its endless hallways; a hundred cousins have curled up in its warm alcoves to read. A woman once died gently in the basement; a dog died gently in the woods. Near that spot one tree rises from the body of another.

I know the bright woods and thickets of the land, the crumbled ruin of stone walls marking lost boundaries. I know these homes: the finches', the pheasants', the starlings', the cardinals', the opossums'. I know the age of one oak tree that lies in tatters down by the marsh: 108. I know where a crow once caught and peeled a squirrel, leaving the skin inside-out amid last year's dry oak leaves.

I know the huge maple tree where the night herons live in late summer. Big-shouldered birds, about two feet tall, they hunch silently in the swaying branches all day, hardly moving at all. At dusk they sail off into the nearby marsh, their huge wings opening like prayers, their hoarse cries harrowing the gathering darkness. They seem as big in flight as startled angels.

If home is in the knowing of stories, I am home.

—B.D.

MILLER'S FOLLY

My father-in-law is buried on a hillside in the Oregon countryside. Around his headstone are cedar and spruce trees; near him sleeps his grandson, who died young. At the bottom of the hill there is a creek that wends south and east, toward a village called Molalla.

In Molalla is the house he built himself. Before there was a house there were blackberry thickets higher than a man's head. To get to the nearby creek you had to bring a sickle. The house took some years to build because he built it on Saturdays and Sundays. He built several porches and a fireplace big enough to roast a bear. He laid in gardens, lawns, hedges, and trees. Because the creek is too shallow for swimming, he dug a pond near it. It would be a cozy swimming hole, he told his wife. He set to work with his sons and grandsons. They dug the hole and cleared away the mud. Instantly, the pond filled with frogs and mud. They lugged the froggy mud away with streaming shovels. The pond immediately filled up again. This went on for some years. Every spring man and boys would attack; the pond would laugh and fill up again with mud and frogs. The pond acquired a family name: Miller's Folly.

Then he died, the house was sold, the family scattered, years passed, I married his final daughter. Recently I went to look at the pond, to find some of the man. It was late afternoon, when the edges of the day turn russet. The pond broke my heart. It is ragged and rife with weeds. Blackberry tangles are everywhere. Cattails obscure the western rim. I stood for a moment, watching swallows carving dusk.

In my mind I told him this was folly; to strive for clarity year after year is madness. He answered me patiently, using his hands to show me the shape of his ambition. His hands were gnarled and deliberate. A mosquito landed on his forehead. His huge ears were silhouetted against the fading light.

I think his soul is here where he fought the mud. I think he is in the voices of children. I think he is not dead, but coursing through water and dreaming in the hearts of green things. I think that stories summon and honor him, and that tales of him are prayers of enormous power.

Also I think his muddy pond is a sacred place.

—B.D.

SPEAKING OREGON

I spend a few days each month at a house on the Oregon coast, in the little village of Neskowin—"many fish," in the Salish tongue once used there by the Tillamook tribe. The beach is open and alluring, but I prefer to walk in the soft rolling hills that crowd along the shore like waves of earth. The hills are cut by old fire roads, logging roads, quarry trails, creeks named for panther and teal. Occasionally I find the pathways of black-tailed deer, which push through the salal thickets like burly teenagers. In these hills and thickets are bears, bobcats, fishers. There is a rumor of cougar, that most graceful language of the remote woods.

Recently I tracked down a topographic map of my Neskowin hills and pinned it up in my office, under my window, which peers out over the river and into the West Hills— the Tualatin Mountains, as a friend of mine calls them. He is an Oregonian, eighty years old, an editor and writer and lumberman all his life. He is a fine man with a face like a piece of bark and a crewcut like a fresh-mown lawn. He came into my office the other day and stared at the map.

"Hemlock in those hills, I bet," he said.

"Some," I said. "Mostly second or third spruce."

"Lot of alder in the cuts?"

"Tons. Salmonberry, too."

"Thickets?"

"Jungles."

He eyed the map for a while, and we talked some more about alder trees, which often curve together in canopies over streambeds. Such alder dries crookedly, in the shape of its original bend; it is called tension alder and is the bane of sawmills, said my friend, who had wandered all through the Pacific Northwest as a lumberman's representative, visiting gyppo outfits and little mills and acquiring an astonishing knowledge of trees and bushes. Talk of alder led him to a discussion of ways to leach the red dye out of the wood, and that led him to a comparison of the tensile strength of hemlock and Douglas fir, and then to cottonwood, which makes the loveliest veneer for plywood. Cottonwood grows best near streams, and talk of streams led us to the water ouzel, or dipper, which lives on the edges of streams and feeds in them and sings like them. Dippers led to bears and elk and owls, all of which have slept in my friend's woods at Arch Cape. The owl, he said, was smoke gray and the size of a child. We talked a while more and then he ambled off, his belly peering between his suspenders like a face between fenceposts.

A minute later I realized that he and I had been speaking Oregonian.

It is his native language, but I have had to learn it from scratch. It has water and wood and wind in it. It has many dialects. Some are the speeches of creatures: bear, heron, glacier, fir. Some are the tongues of tribes—Chinookan, Siuslawan, Molallan, Shapatan, Waiilappuan—tongues once spoken all over the state, oceans of words now dried back to isolated ponds. Now there is Spanish, English, Japanese, Mixtec, city slang. There are dialects of hate; there are stump stories and lovers' lies and the lies we tell each other called politics.

I did not even hear the word *Oregon* until I was eight years old. I discovered a lot of things that year. I discovered, for example, that I lived on an island 33 miles wide and 133 miles long. The island had been called Paumanok for many centuries by the Shinnecock Indians who still lived there. The discovery that I was a Paumanokan was my first taste of geography, and it was a great shock. I was *placed,* so to speak, for the first time; I was given a map much bigger than my boy-maps of yard, street, woods. I was also given a new language, a native tongue with words for the physical island (salt marsh, kettle-hole pond) and its creatures and places: scallops, bluefish, marsh hawks; Copaigue, Patchogue, Montauk.

A week later Sister Marie Aimée told us that our island— unimaginatively rechristened Long Island by its seventeenth-century English and Dutch settlers—was part of a much larger state called New York. She also added that New York was one of *fifty* states. To prove this ludicrous latter thesis she herded us into the school library to research the natural resources, crops, industries, arts, crafts, histories, literatures, populations, and geologies of the United States, one state per child. She put fifty slips of paper in a hat and pulled them forth with a flourish, like tiny rabbits.

The boy in front of me got New York, and did a joyous little touchdown dance at his luck. I was handed Oregon. I remember that the name seemed mysterious and ancient to me, brawny and muscular. A minute later we read the names of our states aloud, a litany of the Union, a poem of America chanted in the fluting voices of children. Oregon was ungainly in my mouth and fell out awkwardly: it opened softly and ended hard, like a love affair gone awry.

Many years passed. I moved from New York to Indiana to Illinois to Massachusetts in the course of my career. I learned more Oregon words: salmon, logger, river, cedar, fir. I learned names, too: Siletz, Trask, Tillamook, Prefontaine, Pendleton, Hazel Hall, Tom McCall. I never did learn the correct pronunciation of the state's name, though, and called it *Ore-a-gone,* like everyone else east of Idaho. So that was the name of the Oregon I did not know, a mythic place on the edge of the known world, as far away as I could imagine.

Then I fell in love with an Oregonian. We courted and married and moved to Oregon and had a daughter and then twin sons, all Oregonians. Now I live in the spacious word I could not say. It is the first word of a green language that is draped over the land like a spell. The land is older than the words, and so there are places where there are no names. The hills and woods and high deserts poke through the language like mountains through mist. The language is made of many dialects: rock, sage, water, wood, wind, blood. Its verbs are stories, and its nouns are the threads of history by which we stitch ourselves to the places we want to call home.

I work on a high bluff over the Willamette River, at a university. The campus comprises some 122 acres. On those acres are trees beyond number, among them basswood, hornbeam, ironwood, madrone, mulberry, myrtle, and redwood. In the oaks by the river there is a hawk's nest. It is a sharp-shinned hawk, I think, a fast hawk of the woods, a gray and dangerous hawk. Perhaps once a week I see the bird rocketing through the spangled oaks as if they were not there and he were slicing through mere fat air. This is a bird of the woodland, familiar with his trees, and I envy him that. I wish I knew the trees of my place as well as he knows his, and could slide among them like water, conscious of their ancient power but confident of my own.

Something about the hawk is Oregon to me. Perhaps it is his unerring sense of direction amid the thick trees. Perhaps it is his silence; I have never heard him utter a sound, and I think silence is a powerful word in the language of this landscape. Perhaps it is his sheer *presence;* there are more hawks in the West than there are in the East.

Five years ago I sat in my study in an ancient wooden house in Massachusetts, a house older than Oregon's statehood, and made a list of reasons to move. I had been offered a job editing a fine magazine in the city where my wife was born and raised. First reason to move: my wife wanted to go, and I love my wife more than I can easily say. Second reason: more hawks. Third reason: great state name, like Idaho or Montana, unlike Washington. Fourth reason: I wanted to go, to my great surprise. I loved Massachusetts, loved it with the abiding passion of an immigrant for the place he or she finds refuge, and I knew my little village by the sea, knew every inch of it, knew where nests and caves and broken boats were. Yet there was a part of me that inexplicably wanted to go West. Perhaps home and away are always at war. Perhaps adventure is a dream that curdles security. Perhaps Americans are indeed a people always leaning west.

"We all play at transporting ourselves new into new country, seeing freshly," writes William Kittredge, who was born in dry Oregon and who talks about storytelling as a means of living deeply, because he is convinced that we can *tell* ourselves home, create stories that become homes, and that home is the place where we are closest to recognizing what is sacred and how we fit into the sacred. By the "sacred" I do not mean religion but spirituality, which has more to do with my elfin children asleep on my shoulder or with the dappled purple grapes that my old neighbor gives me every summer than it does with churches of any brand, although I have great affection for those quiet wooden places. Sometimes the way we fit into the sacred is through the door of a church, but more often it has to do with the round shape of patience.

One of the ways that we see anew is to go to a new place; this is an ancient American urge, as old as the country, and there was some of that in my coming here. In a country that is not that old the Pacific Northwest is still the youngest place, except for Alaska, which is made of imagination and ice and which is still more a place to go to than a place to be. And in a young place there is more room for your story. I lived in

Massachusetts for many years, and the stories of that ancient place are as thick as leaves on the ground, stories of great men and women and battles and ships, stories of love and hate and stone. Those stories fill the streets and libraries and rooms of the dusty old houses on the hills. The people of modern Massachusetts wander among old stories, looking for space in which to sing new ones. There are those who need old stories to live by, who relish a thick past like a thick woods, as places rife with life, and I know whereof I speak, for I am such a man; yet I find in Oregon that I do not regret the loss of the old as much as I revel in the room to be new.

This surprises me, but I am in a new country now, where many things are surprising.

My wife was born here. My children were born here. My father-in-law is buried here, on a high hill under cedar and spruce trees. Like many Oregonians, he was born elsewhere; like many Oregonians, he thought this state was paradise, and he carved its earth with his hands and planted trees and flowers and his heart here. His greatest dream was to build his own home in the countryside. Near the end of his life he did just that, slicing through blackberry thickets with a machete and hammering fir and pine planks into a comfortable home on a creek, in the country town of Mollala. He and his three sons built that house. When he died, his family sold the home and lost some of themselves in the process. I think much of what he was is still there in his house. In fact, I think *he* is there, in the crystal creek and cedar trees, in ways I cannot adequately explain.

My daughter was born in the fall. I carried her from the room in which she was born to another room. She was a prayer in my hands. I was sobbing; she was not. She lay awake for hours. I watched her for those hours, mumbling prayers and poems to her, staring at her newness. At some point she fell asleep. My wife was asleep, too. I went home to sleep, driving slowly past fields, firs, creeks, houses. Above my little girl there was a forest of stars: Pegasus, Cassiopeia, the Pleiades. The night was clear. The stars were swimming. I could not sleep and sat up, thinking of my exhausted courageous wife and my new child, a new word in the world.

So I am woven into Oregon by the lines of my love. I test the lines; I think about living elsewhere, back in the birch woods of New England, perhaps; but then my daughter reaches for my hand and we wander through the grapes and blackberries and cedar trees behind our house, and I revel in the lush language of this land.

Where I live, in the slice of wet Oregon west of the Cascades, there are words and names made of mist layered like gray blankets. I am trying to learn them. I am fitting them in my mouth: the names of friends, fish, birds, plants, towns, hills, streets, the dead. Once I was a boy in a library with a word in my mouth, and now I am a man in the mouth of the word. The word is beautiful and ungainly. It is a story. I am telling a little bit of it. My story is green and there is a fast hawk in it.

—B.D.

OTHER OREGONS

This past summer I attended the Fourth of July parade in Neskowin, Oregon. It is a very small parade: a fire engine, a truck carrying an elderly jazz band, a number of residents dressed in outlandish costumes, excited children on bicycles, sundry dogs, and a truck carrying a man wearing a suit made of tin cans.

The parade winds around the village once and ends up back at the grocery store, where there are speeches and songs and awards. Every year I stand there and sing the songs I know: "The Star Spangled Banner," "You're a Grand Old Flag," "God Bless America." I do not know the Marine and Army Air Corps anthems and so do not sing them. Nor, until recently, did I know the words to "Oregon, My Oregon," which concludes matters with a stately flourish.

Every year, as I hear the many voices around me quavering the state song, I think about Oregon. I did not grow up here, so I had wild ideas of the place: beavers the size of cars, continuous oceans of rain, gargantuan fir forests covering every inch of the state. Then I came here to live and discovered other Oregons, real Oregons: salt-sprayed, dry-dust, black, Siuslawan, Japanese, Vietnamese, Kalapuyan. One Oregon is indeed moist and green and covered with trees of herculean girth; another is a pitted moonscape of smoldering slash piles. One is a booming techno-society fueled by espresso and alert to social, cultural, and environmental concerns; another is populated by scrawny migrant children in cartoon T-shirts and filthy underpants. One is the tiny face of a bloody owl chick nailed to a telephone pole with a spike.

Another is the harrowed face of the madwoman who wanders through my town, carrying her possessions in a tattered grocery bag. Still others are the faces of my friends and family, whose many kindnesses are universities to me.

Last summer, feeling grateful to Oregon for the peace and zest and children I have been given here, I learned the words to the state song. I sang them awkwardly and off-key and with increasing difficulty because, I discovered, there were tears streaming into my beard.

> *Land of the rose and sunshine,*
> *Land of the summer's breeze;*
> *Laden with health and vigor*
> *Fresh from the Western seas,*
> *Blest by the blood of martyrs,*
> *Land of the setting sun;*
> *Hail to thee, Land of Promise,*
> *My Oregon.*

—B.D.

A WAR STORY

My father went to war in March of 1943, just before he was to graduate from Queens College in New York City. An astute and popular young man (he was president of his senior class), he joined the Army and was sent eventually to aerial-intelligence training in Maryland. In October of 1943 he came home on a pass and married my mother. In the summer of 1944 he was made a master sergeant and sent to the Pacific on the troop ship S.S. *Mormacsea*. Neither he nor my mother knew where he was going, and it would be many months before my mother knew that her husband had been assigned to the Americal Division, which had been cut to shreds in battles among the Solomon Islands. The names of two of those islands still chill Pacific War veterans: Guadalcanal, Bougainville.

"Because the censorship was so strict, it was many months before I knew where Jim was," wrote my mother recently. "Letters came, often in bunches, but no place-names or details were allowed." By the time she heard from an uncensored husband, he was in Brisbane, Australia, in an Army intelligence unit attached to Gen. Douglas MacArthur's command. As the Pacific War moved into the Philippines, so did my father, and in June of 1945 he and his unit arrived in Manila. In July he began hearing from Far East Air Force pilots that the war would soon be over. He thought they were crazy. He was working on plans for the invasion of Tokyo on August 6 when an American plane dropped an atomic bomb on Hiroshima.

My father, a photo-reconnaissance expert, was among the

first men to see B-29 photographs of Hiroshima after the bomb exploded. "It seemed that the city had been obliterated," says my father, who chooses his words carefully. Japan opened peace negotiations on August 10, the day after Nagasaki was obliterated. On August 14 Japan accepted surrender terms, and on September 2, in Tokyo Bay, the war ended with a stroke of a pen. Three months later my father boarded the *General John Pope* and came home.

His father, a thoughtful man, had reserved a room at the McAlpin Hotel in New York City for his son, and that is where my father and mother met and resumed their lives in January of 1946. Soon enough another conflict would call, and my father would put his uniform on again, but for the moment his war was over.

He was twenty-four years old.

—B.D.

THE TIES THAT BIND

In my house, which is small and white and wooden, there is a woman, a man, a girl, a shrew, an orange tree, two baby boys, nine spiders, a flock of fruit flies, and several dozen honey ants, the remnants of several hundred that until very recently lived in the basement and made regular forays in orderly lines up the stairs and into the kitchen, where they fastidiously held out for honey and jelly and adamantly refused the spoonfuls of peanut butter so generously proffered them by my daughter, who enjoys their company, and who has taken to laying thin lines of honey across the kitchen in lovely patterns, including once a portrait of her father, who watched, awed, daughter in lap, as the lines of his face were populated slowly by ants hardly bigger than bits of sand.

This bit of sweet theater made me think uncomfortably of the way that my face will someday be a highway for invertebrates when my body is no longer animated by the odd spirit that drives it today, but it also led me to ponder the ways in which my house is a thriving community of creatures, invited and uninvited, all dining on my dollar. Some are there by accident: the shrew fell through an open basement window and landed foursquare on a copy of Edward Gibbon's *The Decline and Fall of the Roman Empire,* which dazed the shrew, to the surprise of no one who has worked upstream against the cascade of Gibbonian sentences. Others, like the spiders and the boys, were born there, and have known no other home, and occasionally share the same diet, specifically beetles, which the boys are wonderfully quick at downing, to the dismay, I assume, of the spiders, not to mention the beetles.

Thus we are bound by humor and beetles, by honey and spider silk, and by universal astonishment at the shrew, which could not be tamed, but was turned out into the yard to thin the herds of crickets, which it did with wonderful dispatch, that being the nature of shrews. As it scrabbled away into the brush I felt a pang of loss, for the shrew was one of us for a time, a stitch in the fabric of our family; and I thought, not for the first time, that we are each threaded to one another by love, thorough or insufficient, inexplicable and necessary, as ephemeral and savory as lines of honey, as the lines on the face of God.

—B.D.

PART 3

THE HOLY ROMAN CATHOLIC CHURCH

R eligion *is* literature, as that sensible man George Santayana once remarked, and the Catholic faith, perhaps more than any other, depends on story: the miraculous birth in a hovel, the prescient child, the thin bearded man telling puzzling parables on the roads of Judea; a murder against a slate-gray sky, and then an immense boulder rolled away from the cave as if it were a pebble, and the Son of God risen from the vaults of the dead. From the stories of that most paradoxical man, Jesus Christ of Nazareth, lord of the star fields, has come the paradoxical, magical, ludicrous faith that has riveted both authors all their lives. Here then are essays about Christ, Catholicism, and "the lines on the face of God."

THE LOQUACIOUS MAN

I have been a Catholic since 1956, when I was baptized wearing a white dress. My forebears, family, friends, schools, and employers were Catholic. Catholicism was my language, my coat, my house. I learned to pray in two American Catholic tongues, Latin and English, and to relish the smoky poetry of the Mass, an ancient ritual prayer. I chanted the rosary with my brothers and sister, I prayed to Saint Francis when I found the huddled corpses of sparrows, I prayed to Saint Blaise when my throat burned. When I was twelve, my grandmother shriveled and died and I prayed desperately for her soul during her funeral Mass, a sad waltz that taught me the enormous power of ritual, the skeleton that sustains us when we are weak.

Then I stopped praying. It seemed pointless, a speech delivered to an empty room, a plea without ears.

Many years passed. I grew up. Slowly, I began to hear and see and taste prayers: a fox against snow, my wife's hand, my mother's corduroy voice. One morning on an island I went to get my mail and two purple finches flew out of the mailbox and I knew that they were prayers. One day, years later, a cold doctor said to me, "You will never have children," and that night I opened my mouth and prayed to the woods and skies and birds, to the shambling God I could not find but sensed everywhere, and since that day I have prayed silently and aloud, with my hands and feet, with my heart.

It seems to me now that all things are prayers. Curiosity and memory and silence and water are prayers. People are prayers. I have a daughter now, two years old, an exuberant prayer. We talk about God, whom she calls Gott. When she is asleep, my wife and I cover her with one blanket and two prayers.

As a boy I learned the names of the boxes that prayers are mailed in: the Our Father, the Hail Mary, the Mass of the Dead. I came to hate the boxes because they seemed empty, mere strings of dusty words. I did not see that they are a means to an end, and that the end is a piercing conversation with Gott, the man who is nowhere and everywhere, who is not a man, who was a man, who never stops talking.

—B.D.

Two Angels

I was twelve years old when I first saw an angel. There were two of them. They were in the attic of my house in New York. They were perhaps eight or ten feet tall. Their wings were larger than their bodies. Their bodies and clothes were of a white material that looked something like stone. Their feet were shod. Their faces were cold and although they did not look directly at me I sensed that they knew I was there. I was so scared I wet my pants.

I stumbled out of the attic and ran down the stairs to my sister's room. She held me while I cried. I told her about the angels and she understood and held me some more. She is a good sister, although she doesn't hold me as much anymore, now that we are much older and she is in a Buddhist monastery.

Buddhists do not believe in angels as such, but they do believe there are spirits that influence earthly matters. So do Hindus. So do Taoists. Mormons, named for an angel named Moroni, believe that there are angels. Jews believe that there are angels. Muslims believe that every soul has angels that chronicle good and bad deeds. Zoroastrians believe that there are *Fravashis*—guardian angels.

Christians believe that there are angels. Catholics believe that there are nine hosts of angels arrayed in descending order of rank from the throne of the Lord: seraphim, cherubim, thrones, dominations, virtues, powers, principalities, archangels, and guardian angels, according to the sixth-century monk Dionysus the Areopagite. Saint Albert the Great estimated that there were 399,920,004 angels in those ranks. (Jewish cabalists of the Middle Ages counted slightly fewer:

301,655,722.) Scripture itself mentions only three, but those are the three greatest: Michael, Gabriel, and Raphael, whose names mean He who is like God, He who is God's strength, and He who is God's healing.

A friend of mine named Christy Stotler once told me a riveting story about angels. Christy is an ethereal young woman who lives in Boston. She was raised in South Africa and came to the United States to go to college. She was raised on a farm outside the town of Louis Frichardt, in the foothills of the Soutpansberg Mountains, about one hundred kilometers south of the South Africa–Zimbabwe border. Louis Frichardt is about a day's drive south of Harare, the capital of Zimbabwe, and a day's drive north of Johannesburg, South Africa's largest city; during the Rhodesian War (1970–80), the little town became a convenient stop for military convoys traveling back and forth between the two countries.

Civilians traveled with the convoys for protection, said Christy, and her home quickly became a sort of underground-railway stop for travelers—"first Nazarene missionaries [her parents were Nazarene missionaries], then missionaries from other denominations, then friends of missionaries, then friends of friends, then acquaintances of friends, then strangers," Christy explained.

One group of travelers going to Johannesburg told Christy that their convoy had gone through an area rumored to be a guerrilla target. The convoy crawled along the road, and soldiers walked in advance to check for land mines. The tension was palpable; trouble was expected. "My friends began to pray for the Lord's protection," said Christy. "As they looked up from their prayers, a column of angels was seen stretching forward and behind the convoy, flanking the road on either side, a towering winged wall. I cannot recall how long the angels were visible to them or whether they were armed for battle or not.

"I do not believe that culture and tradition create the supernatural," wrote Christy recently, "but I do believe that culture can foster eyes to see what is unseen. I grew up in Africa, where people believe in the existence and importance of both the seen and the unseen worlds."

I am not sure what I think about the unseen world, but I do know that I saw two angels once. They were bigger than the room itself, if that makes sense. I don't know how that could be, but that was my impression. They seemed to *loom*— that's the best word. I noticed them out of the corner of my eye as I was searching for something amid the old baseball bats and fishing poles and other detritus of a large family in a small house. There was a flutter, and I turned to look and saw and heard them hammering their wings against the walls. It seemed to me that they were unhappy, or at least not happy—perhaps they were not capable of emotion and had just been caught unaware in the attic.

Years later while attempting to write about this experience I resorted to fiction, speculating that perhaps they were curious about mortality and wanted to taste it and had somehow miscalculated and become stuck for a time in an attic; but this is a fanciful idea, and I don't have any real reason to think it's true. It's enough to try to honestly describe the experience of seeing two angels in my attic when I was twelve years old.

It's important to explain how normal my attic and house and family were. The attic was a room fifteen feet deep by ten feet wide, with sharply sloping ceilings. My father, a tall man, could walk upright down the center of the room but had to stoop on the sides. A boy of twelve could stand upright. The room itself was dark and musty and was lit with a single naked light bulb. A long string hung from the bulb's short metal chain, so when you opened the door and confronted the darkness you fished nervously for the string, casting your hands into the air like birds, waiting for the flickering kiss of the string. The room smelled brown and old. It was lined with old brown paper over thick insulation. Stacked against the walls were old mattresses and box springs and a folded crib; filling most of the rest of the space were fishing rods, baseball bats, tennis rackets, pillows, sheets, blankets, coats, jackets, table leaves, hats, gloves, books. I wish I could remember everything in that room, but I can't.

The house was built in 1930 or so. My parents bought it in 1955. They still live there. Over the course of those years my father built rooms for his children in the basement and on the second floor. It's a small house but very comfortable; there are a lot of places in it, and a child wanting to hide or read can easily find a corner in which to do so. My family is gentle and friendly. The occupations of the five children are, in order, mathematician, Buddhist nun, journalist, cabinet-maker, and grade-school vice principal. I'm the journalist. I followed in the footsteps of my father, a journalist since 1946, when he was discharged from the U.S. Army. My mother was a teacher and a housewife. She still teaches people to read. She's a very good teacher.

My parents are devout Catholics, and several of us children are Catholic, but we were Catholics in the usual sense— quiet Catholics, civilized Catholics, Catholics who made a strenuous effort to treat others well and to see the divine in all things, but not Catholics so enamored of the odd trappings of the faith that we spoke in tongues or saw the Virgin Mary's face in the maple trees out back. As for angels, we believed in them but did not expect to see them in the attic. Yet when I told my sister and parents that I had seen two angels in the attic, they were calm about the matter. I think now that my family knew then that miracles probably arrive in our world in this quiet fashion, news of them coming by report of a child, or by the unusual actions of pets, or by a clock running backward.

The poet William Blake saw angels as a child, several times. At age ten he reported that he had seen a tree filled with angels, their "bright angelic wings bespangling every bough like stars." His father beat him. A month later, as he stood at the edge of a field, watching haymakers at work, he saw angels walking toward him through the rye. His parents stopped beating him and sent him to art school.

My parents didn't do anything special after I saw two angels in the attic. My mom washed out my wet underwear and dried it and folded it and put it in my chest of drawers— an act of kindness she must have performed many thousands of times for her children. My dad came upstairs with me when I went to bed. He did not tell me stories or pretend that what I had seen was a dream. He just sat there on the edge of the bed, rubbing my back until I fell asleep, and then I suppose he rose quietly and checked on my sleeping brothers and turned out the light and softly went downstairs—quiet acts that he must have performed thousands of times, too.

Last night I was rubbing my little daughter's back as she fell asleep, and I remembered my father's huge calm hand on my own thin back, many years ago. When my little girl fell asleep, I covered her with a blanket and padded quietly out of her room. As I closed her door I was overwhelmed by the many years of love that my parents had lavished on me and that I returned poorly if at all until I was a man. I wanted to tell them that I love them enormously, but now I live thousands of miles away.

Some months ago I was back in the old house with all of my brothers. I went up to the attic late one afternoon and opened the door. The angels were gone. I fished for the string of the light bulb, waving my hands like wings, and I wondered where they went.

—B.D.

THE GAUNT MAN

Years ago, on a wet Easter morning, I found a fallen sparrow chick on the concrete floor of the garage. It was a male, about a week old. He was twisted, small, deceased. Sometime during the night he had fallen or been shoved by his siblings from a disheveled nest in the eaves. My brothers and I buried him in a crayon box and prayed over the gaudy coffin. My youngest brother sobbed convulsively. The broken chick did not rise from the dead, as we hoped but did not expect. Ever after, says my brother, he looked upon Jesus with a jaundiced eye, and questioned the potency of a story that could not stir life in something so small as a shriveled sparrow.

I have wondered at that story, too. It was the epic of my youth: a magic birth on a crystalline night, a precocious boy in a temple, water and blood, a dusty murder on a dark afternoon—and the final thrilling detail, an *empty tomb* where the dead man had been, its huge stone door flung aside like a pebble.

It was the first story I knew well, the first tale in which I could hear the clash and ring of history and sin. Its hero—gaunt, wrapped in a long white cloak, dusty feet in dusty sandals—fascinated me, and I studied his legend, pored over the disparate accounts of his brief life, strained to hear divine music in his odd stories. I tried, fitfully, to emulate his patience, generosity, and courage. But mostly, as I grew older and more suspicious of magic, I forgot him, although he hovered at the edge of consciousness and memory, sad-faced and haunted, a gaunt bearded man who died young and was probably God.

Not until I turned thirty-three did I finally taste the sour evil of his death on my tongue, and sense the real horror of his murder. For a Catholic boy, that age is one of power and resonance, of inevitable measurement against that lost life, of stock taken; and over the course of that year I found myself thinking about the carpenter more than I expected to and more than I wanted to. I found myself staring at his story in the oddest moments: on the train, in the woods, in the cobbled alleys of my ancient city. I couldn't get over the stark fact of his death, which stuck out like the ribs of a malnourished child.

A quiet carpenter is arrested, spiked to a cross, and left to die. Dust and a strange darkness swirl at his feet. His mother weeps; his best friend watches in helpless silence. Twilight crawls over the nearby hills. He cries aloud with thirst, despair, terror; and he dies. Three days later he is seen on the road. He walks, he talks, he allows a skeptic to plunge a thumb into his wounds. He disappears again, but this time the fierce story of his life and death remains in the air, outlined by the blood and tears of those who knew him. The story spreads and takes on a life of its own, filling the earth. Two thousand years later the carpenter's story, unaccountably powerful, still haunts the world.

And it haunts me.

Stories are powerful, weighty things. They have lives of their own. Woven of memory and desire, they begin with an ungainly parade of facts in the same way that a sparrow chick is made up of downy uncertainty, splayed feet, and hunger. With time they acquire grace beyond their ingredients, and meaning beyond the hole they occupy in the freighted air.

I have my own story, in which compassion and mercy and humor salve a little of the evil I find in my city, in my work, in the twisted people and ashen faces that pass me in the street. In my middle years I look for God in the carved faces of my elders and the translucent faces of the young, in joy and sadness, in gain and loss, in the eyes of fish, the boles of oaks, the runes left by the feet of birds. I have fled from the crutch of faith, the evil of religion too tightly held, the intolerance of the confident, because it is subtlety that seems holy to me, not assurance; because those men and women most sure of themselves and their gods often seem furthest removed from godlike peace and mercy.

But always the carpenter's story whispers to me. It is as haunting as love, as persistent as doubt. For years I have dodged in and out of it like a child on the bright thin edge of a forest, immersed in it when it suited me, ignoring it when it did not. Now I face it with awe and fear and pity. In the piping voices of children, in the hollow voices of beggars, in the savage barking of guns in alleys I hear the ragged voice of the man on the cross, raging at his betrayal, offering his broken soul to the harsh God he called his father.

I don't know if that man was the lord of time and space and mercy. No one knows; no one will ever know, not in this life. You bet your life on him or you don't; you walk into his story, wondering at its astonishing power, leery of its simplicity and enormous demand, or you walk away from it because it is impossible to believe or live by. Like a mountain, a cathedral, a sparrow, the story of the gaunt man is a vaulting thing, impossible to ignore.

I am afraid of his story because I suspect that it is true.

—B.D.

THE WATERS OF LIFE

S ome weeks ago my wife delivered two sons into the world. When they were six days old, a priest came to our house and baptized them on the dining-room table. He poured water from the Jordan River over their heads. The water trickled over their brows and fell into a large porcelain bowl. Liam, the younger boy by a minute, slept through his baptism, but his brother, Joseph, was awake, riveted by the flaring candles on the table. When the water from the river in which Jesus Christ was baptized slid across Joseph's head, he urinated with such abandon that his father's right hand, clamped over the boy's crotch for secure handling, was soaked. His father, already deeply moved by the simplicity and power of the ancient ritual, silently made note of yet another water binding and haunting the gathered company, and dried his hand with a dishtowel when the rite was finished.

For baptism is a matter of many waters. There were tears on my mother's face as she stood next to my father, the two of them rapt with memories of the baptisms of their own children. I saw water sparkle on the brown fox face of my oldest son and the ruddy round face of his brother. The priest's enormous hands glistened with water, as they had glistened many hundreds of times before over the many hundreds of children he had baptized. The many waters of Oregon's autumn rains lashed the windows. I watched my tired lovely small strong wife in the flickering light; from her salty waters had come these boys, formed in her silent sea and then with bawls and blood sent swimming toward the light; and here we were, on their first Sunday, mothers and fathers and broth-

ers and cousins and friends and godparents, gathered to bring
these boys closer to the Light.

It is an ancient ritual, older by far as a cleansing rite than
Christianity, traceable within Christianity to Jesus himself,
who stood in the Jordan and had its waters poured upon him
by a true believer—a curious and prickly soul so sure that
baptism was a means toward salvation that his name has
descended to us as John the Baptist. He wanted to be clean,
Jesus did. He wanted to get a clean start, to wipe the slate of
everything but love; and he asked John to baptize him with
the running waters of a river, that most relentless of scouring
creatures.

"I need to be baptized by you, and do you come to me?"
(Matthew 3:14) asked John, astonished John, savage and rude
John, John who had just baptized Pharisees and Sadducees
while audibly gritting his teeth and lashing them with his
razor tongue in a speech that began "You brood of vipers!"
and then got less polite, John of the "clothing of camel's hair
with a leather belt around his waist, and his food was locusts
and wild honey," as Matthew reported in his gospel (3:4–7).

"Let it be so now," said Jesus, equably, "for it is proper
for us in this way to fulfill all righteousness" (3:15). And so
on his brow John poured the waters of the Jordan, the mighty
river of Judea.

"And when Jesus had been baptized," wrote Matthew, the
careful reporter anxious to get all the details of the scene
down correctly, "just as he came up from the water, suddenly
the heavens were opened to him and he saw the Spirit of God
descending like a dove and alighting on him. And a voice
from heaven said, 'This is my Son, the Beloved, with whom I
am well pleased'" (3:16–17).

A sentiment I felt myself, after my boys were baptized;
and I looked across the room and saw my own father smiling

at one of his five beloved sons, in whom he was well pleased. And I thought again, for the hundredth time that day, how baptism especially is the sacrament of time, the rite that bends time like a toy, the ritual that shames time and robs it, for an elastic moment, of its awful power. I am bound to my sons by waters; I am bound to my beloved elfin daughter by the waters and words that broke across her head three years ago; I am again for an instant the child in my parents' arms nearly forty years ago in a church near the sea, in the same crackling-clean white dress into which my son Joseph is urinating with such joyous force this day. So as my sons are anointed with water and oil and welcomed into the company of believers, I am thinking of my own anointing, and that of my mother, baptized in New York, and of my father, baptized in Pittsburgh, and of the line of baptisms stretching back to Ireland and Germany, all those squalling infants cradled in the arms of their parents and godparents deep into the past, and all those waters running back to Christ waist-deep in the roaring waters of the Jordan, with John's muscular arm crooked over his head, pouring water, lovely quicksilver magic pure water; it slips off his brow and splashes back into the river, which roars away to the sea.

One of the reasons that I believe the itinerant preacher and sometime carpenter's assistant Jesus Christ of Nazareth was indeed the Lord of stars and souls is that his story is so often cryptic and puzzling. This seems to me the mark of a true thing, and in my desultory reading of the New Testament I am often struck by the sheer oddness of his remarks, the oblique metaphors and similes, the consistent reversal of expectations. That the last shall be first makes no sense, but that is the way it will be, said Christ, flatly. Various men work in a vineyard for varying times and all are paid the same wage; this makes no sense, but that is what the love of the Father is like, said Christ. He reached for metaphors that hint at the inexplicable; and so his stories and remarks are often ambiguous and puzzling.

As is his remark to John on the bank of the river. "It is proper for us in this way to fulfill all righteousness," said Christ, calmly—an ornate and somewhat legalistic remark from a man hiking up his robe with both hands and stepping gingerly into the sucking mud and icy shock of a river. Did he mean that this cleansing event was right and proper at this time in his career, or was he sighing and saying the rite must be performed simply to fulfill the expectations of the multitudes gathered by the river?

Both, I think; Christ was always keenly aware of his role as the Expected One, the One who would fulfill prophecies, and so he permitted John to christen him with clear waters so that he might be in accordance with what was expected of him, the man whom John proclaimed (probably at the top of his brawling voice) the Lamb of God. But I also think that Christ wanted to be baptized at that moment, wanted to make a formal statement about the advent of a new covenant, in which the first act of a life would be a blessing by water, and the cleansing of sins.

And I cannot help thinking that the human being who was Jesus of Nazareth wanted almost desperately to stand under the cascade of his cousin's fervor, and be shriven of his own fear and pride; for in that odd Nazarene, both God and un- employed laborer, blind terror of his impending murder, which he foresaw all too clearly, and a fierce furious pride that he was himself the Messiah, born to save all souls, must always have been at war. I think that the man must have had thou- sands of Gethsemanes, thousands of evil nights of the soul.

In Mark's Gospel, John the Baptist "appeared in the wilder- ness, proclaiming a baptism of repentance *for the forgive-*

ness of sins" (1:4; italics mine), and baptism to this day carries that duty as well as being the means by which men and women are welcomed into the community of believers, into the story of the risen Christ. Before the Second Vatican Council directed that the communal aspect of baptism be reemphasized, the rite's role in wiping away original sin had a greater emphasis, and the destination of those children who died before being baptized was a name all Catholic schoolchildren were taught: Limbo. This was, it should be noted, a pious tradition, not a doctrine, and it made a certain cold sense, if one believes that by virtue of the bodies we wear we are clothed with sin, and that baptism's greatest sacramental power is the removal of that sin.

I believe that my sons are liable to sin, and certain to commit it, and greatly blessed if they have the humility and grace to confess it and by doing so be shriven, even as I know that I have sinned, and sin daily, and have sinned ten thousand times despite my feeble efforts to avoid doing so; but I do not believe that *they* have sinned, not yet, poor suckling lambs, and if they had died in our arms before they were blessed with water and oil on that wet Sunday at the dining-room table, no man and no woman and no Church could convince me that they did not rejoin their awesome Maker. It is evil to say so, a cruel injury upon the parents, and the fading of nonsense like Limbo is a mark of the grace of which our human Church is occasionally capable. That sputtering grace, in fact, is why I belong to the Church, and why my wife and I brought our sons and daughter to it; we want them to be members of a community that every so often sees a blinding light, and has the wit and heart to struggle toward it, past and through what seems sensible.

Mark, too, reported the voice of the Father crackling out of heaven immediately after Christ's baptism; and then Mark noted tersely that "the Spirit immediately drove him out into the wilderness" (1:12), where he would thrash about for forty days, wrestling with the devil.

In our case the Spirit impelled my son Joseph to the changing table to be swaddled in a dry diaper and a coat of many colors, and it sent Liam into the capacious arms of his grandfather, where he nestled like an acorn in an oak. The boys' dazed father was impelled to go out into the wilderness in front of his house, where he stood silently amid the riotous growth of cedars, firs, pines, hawthorns, hazelnuts, and hollies in his yard. In his hand was the old porcelain bowl into which the waters of the Jordan had fallen after they had blessed the souls of his new sons. With his right hand he blessed himself, slowly, and then he turned to the four directions and flicked a little water to each, and then he poured the rest of the water on the roots of the cedar tree and went back inside the house, where the many waters in the teakettle were coming to a boil.

—B.D.

An Ancient Promise

My friend Thomas became a priest when he was twenty-eight years old. Before he donned the "crow suit," as he calls his cassock, he was a physical therapist with a sweet Southern girlfriend. One summer day he packed his old car with his gear and drove to a seminary. Five years later he was an assistant pastor in a Memphis slum. Since then he's served stints in parishes in Chicago and New York; today, at age thirty-six, he is the chaplain of a New York hospital.

He is on call twenty-four hours a day and his face shows it. There are gray hairs in his beard and he smokes two packs of cigarettes a day. He lives in two rooms with two birds. He is at the same time the most direct and the most gentle man I know. He has been at the bedside of dying children more times than he can remember.

"What do you tell them?" I asked.

"That God will hold them in his hands," he said.

"How can you stand it?" I asked.

"Someone has to take care of their souls."

A few months after he packed his car and drove to the seminary we were drinking old whiskey together on Christmas Eve, a tradition we followed for many years. We met every year in a bar under a railroad track. When a freight went over, the bottles jumped and startled behind the bar; sometimes the jukebox would shut itself off.

"Why do you want to be a priest?" I asked.

"Because my guts said so."

"What the hell does that mean?"

"I don't know, Brian," said Tom patiently. "I just know

this is what I should do. I believe that people have souls, and that their souls are eternal, and that what they do on earth matters enormously. I believe that there are men and women who give up one life to help people with that other life, and I think I'm one of those men. I never cared much for the formal Church, for the politics and rituals and regulations, but there is something deep in the priesthood, something inarticulate, something that stabs me in the heart. You can't dress it up in words because words fall off it. It's ancient and holy. Let's drink to it."

I did, and I do.

—B.D.

GODFATHERING

It is one of the graces of my life that I have three times been asked to be a godfather, twice for nephews and once for the daughter of dear friends. In fact I am the co-godfather of this delightful young lady, and at her baptism, some years ago, we godfathers held her suspended between us like a tiny chicken, each man holding a goddaughterly wing, and so, angelically and airily, she was received into the Church.

In addition to godfathering three children I am blessed to be the father of three more, also two boys and a girl, and in this capacity I have, in concert with my wife, asked friends and family to be the godparents of our children. Each time the choice was carefully weighed and made, and just as carefully and respectfully accepted. Just a few months ago my wife and I asked two men and two women to be the godparents of our new sons, and while the custom is fresh in my mind I would like to stare it full in the face for a moment and ponder its odd power and import in a modern Catholic life.

Like many Catholic traditions, the roots of godparenting are mysterious. One theory is that the custom is traceable to the Roman Empire, in which Christianity began and from which the faith drew many of its habits. In that august society there was little vertical mobility; social roles were very much defined by station, and so patrons or benefactors from the class above were much sought after, especially for children. A good father would very much wish to have his child "related" to a powerful or prestigious patron. When the empire became officially Christian, the habit of patronage took on a theological cast, and so, goes the theory, began the practice of designating godparents at baptism.

Another theory is that godparenting arose from a pre-Christian practice of designating spiritual relatives. Among many ancient peoples (the Celts in Europe and the Salish in North America, for example), parents would ask one or more members of the clan to pay special attention to the spiritual growth of a new child. Among many North American peoples, a child would also be given a spiritual cousin among the local fauna: sometimes the clan's totem animal, sometimes a creature for which the child developed a special affection or respect. In Europe, at least, where the English language developed from Germanic roots, the habit of godparenting is evident in the language itself. The original meaning of the word *gossip* was "God-sibling," and a godparent was considered to have such a close spiritual relationship with a godchild that the Church at one time forbade a godparent and godchild from marrying each other.

Four years ago my wife and I chose godparents for our first child. We had considered candidates, idly, as we had idly considered names for our child, but, like naming Lily, the actual choice of godparents was surprisingly hard because we took it very seriously. In the end we asked my brother and my wife's sister to "help train Lily in the practice of the faith, and bring her up to keep God's commandments as Christ taught us, and to love God and our neighbors," in the words of the celebrant. And so Lily's godparents stood beside us as we renounced Satan and his works and his empty promises, and rejected sin and the glamour of evil, and affirmed belief in the Father and the Son and the Spirit, the communion of saints, the forgiveness of sins, the resurrection of the body, and life everlasting; and then with us they held squirming Lily as water cascaded across her head and a prayer (called *ephphatha*) was said over her ears and mouth, that she might receive the Word and proclaim the faith.

Again in recent months we carefully selected godparents, and stood with them as our sons were brought formally into the faith. Again I was struck by the import of the choice, and by how seriously the godparents took their duty; and again I was moved to consider my own role and actions as godfather. Ostensibly, I am to be a moral anchor, to provide spiritual assistance to the instruction of the parents, but this is too pat, too cold and formal, and I have decided that what I am really supposed to do is *be there*—if not physically, then emotionally. I try to visit, write letters, call, send small gifts, surprise these boys and this girl with attentions from a man not ordinarily in their orbit. Some of that attention is avowedly spiritual—I send one godson an annual moral rule (don't punch your sister, don't throw rocks at cars, pray while walking, that sort of thing), but most of it is something else, and it is in the something else that the true practice and power of godparenting lies, I think.

I try to *give,* pure and simple, because I think that attention is love and love is divine. I am not the father of my godchildren; I am the assistant father, and my job is to love them quietly and well. So I give what I can as often as I can.

It was the writer Dorothy Parker who once ably summed up the job of a godparent in a poem called, suitably, "Godmother"; the godmother in that succinct poem gives her goddaughter "sadness, and the gift of pain, the new-moon madness, and the love of rain," among other subtle presents. I might quibble with that litany of gifts, and aim to give other sorts, but I much admire the giving, and I think it the essence of this ancient and modern and lovely and powerful Catholic habit.

—B.D.

A Mass for Maureen
in Her "Village" Church

Sister Maureen Williams died last week and went to heaven. She was the librarian at St. Gregory's School on West 90th Street. She had had some kidney problems recently, then an infection, and in the middle of what we understand was a fairly routine surgical procedure, her heart stopped.

Maureen, our niece, was a Sister of Charity, not yet thirty-five years old. The wake and visiting were held at the Sisters of Charity Center at Mount St. Vincent College in Riverdale. Then, Friday evening, the members of her several families—natural and religious—drove in a twenty-four–car procession, hazard lights flashing, along Riverdale Avenue, along Henry Hudson Parkway, and across to St. Gregory's Church, which was packed with parishioners and ablaze with life, as we came to celebrate her death.

Father Bob Springer, a Jesuit priest who came to know and love Maureen when she lived in the House of Prayer on 97th Street, was there to celebrate the Mass. He recalled that he had been privileged to celebrate Mass two years ago at Maureen's second religious profession, when she entered the Sisters of Charity community after some years in the Newburgh Dominican community.

Father Springer told us that Maureen—a sort of country girl from Connecticut—considered New York City her village. We know that to be true; she used to take her two red-headed nephews from Bristol, Connecticut, to stay with her for a vacation in the city every year. They would have a grand time, learning something new every year about Maureen's village.

She fell in love with New York and its places and people—especially its poor and hurting people. This week she was supposed to start helping out with the soup kitchen project in which she had become involved—POTS (Part of the Solution). The priest who runs it told us that the very afternoon he heard of Maureen's death, when he was wondering how he might possibly get on without her, another woman suddenly appeared and volunteered to take her place.

Father John Lennon, the pastor of St. Gregory's, was at the Mass also. He told us that Maureen would take the children of the school, especially those in trouble with school discipline, into her library and shut the door, closing out, for a time, the painful world outside.

After the Mass, Father Lennon took us upstairs to visit her library. There was still a big pile of books the children had left on the table in the middle of the room. In this little room, she had opened up hundreds of minds and hearts to the wonders of the world of books, films, and records and her own marvelous stories, which she was always inventing and telling the children.

Sister Eileen Storey, a Sister of Charity, was there to give a eulogy. She told us of the classic stories Maureen loved to tell and retell. One was the story of three starving French soldiers who came to a little village and asked for food, and then taught the villagers (who had hidden all their food) how to make soup from just three smooth stones—by borrowing just a small carrot here, some salt there, a bit of beef, a few small potatoes—until there was somehow enough soup for everyone. Just as Maureen had taught the inhabitants of her village to share their lives and love.

Sister Storey said that Maureen learned about cooking from her father, Ed Williams, just as she learned to handle children from her mother, Betty. Ed and Betty were there in the front pew, shattered by her death but understanding and proud that this ending, for Maureen, was the beginning. Ed said to me later that the sadness is only superficial. What counts is the joy of knowing that Maureen is with the Lord.

Maureen's brothers and sisters were there—Paul, Monica, Susan, and Dennis—and Monica's husband, Rit, and their sons, and Su's husband, Dave, and Dennis's wife, Doris. Anne-Marie, the youngest sister, couldn't come from California because she is seven months pregnant, but Ed is going out to be with her this week. Paul and Su and Dave, who live out there, too, will be going with him.

Maureen, their big sister, gave them the stable rallying point they all needed, by her clear purpose of serving God and his people. A lot of the problems her brothers and sisters had had seem to have been straightened out now, and maybe that's why the Lord felt she was ready to be called to him, though ultimately the timing of her death is a mystery.

What was not mystery, though, was the resounding love, the great outpouring of affection for Maureen at last Friday night's Mass at St. Gregory's. All the children she loved from the school were there, and many of their parents and other parishioners. The kids were scrubbed and shining and on their best behavior. The church sparkled with the colorful diversity of that vibrant parish in the heart of Maureen's New York village.

Throughout the Mass, on the top step before the altar sat a small pot of brave, little, snowdrop flowers that our daughter Betsy, Maureen's cousin, had dug up from our front yard that afternoon. Just coming alive again for spring, those tiny flowers told us what we all knew: in the face of death, we come to understand life.

Maureen was affirming it for all of us—going off joyfully to meet the Lord, and we were giving her our best, thankful send-off for the trip.

—J.D.

MISSION AMERICA

A dear friend of ours, a kind and holy priest from Kerala state in India, who served for many years in our parish but has since moved on to another assignment, used to go back home to India every summer for vacation.

On his return here he would tell us with great joy how his family had welcomed him back warmly, what a great visit he'd had, and how proud his mother was that her son was a priest serving in the missions in America.

He always said it with a smile, and we thought it was amusing, but that story also tells us a lot about the Church in the United States these days. To a certain extent—especially in the summer now—ours is becoming a mission Church.

Every year, hundreds, maybe even thousands, of priests from Africa, India, South America, and elsewhere come here to help out in our parishes, where the shortage of priests becomes more and more severe all the time.

In our parish, in addition to our friend Father Aaron from Kerala (who encourages us to call him Aaron because his Indian family name is too long and complicated for us Americans to handle), in recent years we have had three visiting priests from other parts of India, several others from Ghana, Kenya, and elsewhere in Africa, one from Sri Lanka, one from Northern Ireland, another from the Republic of Ireland, and an Irish mission society priest up from Brazil.

From visiting other parishes and talking to their parishioners, we conclude that it's very much the same all across our diocese (Rockville Centre); there must be dozens of priests from all over the world here for the summer or fall. Anywhere from 10 percent to a quarter of the priests in our diocese this summer will be from overseas, I would guess.

Some are here to study for a few months or more, and they live and help in a parish while going to a university. Some others are here just for a while to help out, raising a little money for their diocese back home, their religious order, or some other good purpose.

It is, as they say, a sea change—or maybe one should say an overseas change—in the clergy supply for American parishes.

We have always had priests from overseas among us, of course—mostly from Ireland. When I first went to work for the Catholic Press Association back in the late '50s, I was amazed at how many Irish priests I met in the southern United States, for example. At one meeting in Biloxi, Mississippi, I met more priests speaking with an Irish accent than with a Southern drawl.

Those were permanent transfers, of course—the result of some vigorous visits to Ireland by American bishops who signed up Irish priests to staff their new dioceses. And thank God they came; the Church here has benefited greatly from the infusion of these Irish priests, their holiness, their leadership, their charm, and their love of God.

But today's influx is different. Now we are blessed by the arrival of priests from all over the world. And we have been told that Asia, Africa, South and Central America, and the Near and Far East are where the growth of the Church is strongest, where the future of the Church lies.

We can see the truth of that forecast already, as our visiting priests come among us, helping us to hear the gospel and learn about our faith from different voices, different cultures, different hearts.

Their very presence among us proves the variety yet universality of the Church. They bring unique talents and refreshing approaches to the liturgy and God's word. They broaden us and our native parish priests, helping us all learn about other people and other needs.

Sometimes, even when speaking English, our visitors' accents are a little hard to fathom. But if we try hard enough we understand them. One of our recent visitors, Father Richard from Ghana, after a slow start in getting used to us and we to him, turned out to be a fervent preacher whose every homily was an inspiration. Others are models of humility and holiness. We appreciate them and their special gifts and their generosity in coming among us, and we thank God for sending them to us.

—J.D.

"NEVER SHAVE A CAT" AND OTHER RULES OF LIFE

Our senior grandson, now fully and officially named Neal Andrew James Doyle, was confirmed recently, in a beautiful big parish church in one of Chicago's blooming suburbs.

His godfather, our son Brian, couldn't get to the Midwest for the occasion, so he sent me a letter to pass along to Neal when we were there for the ceremony and I acted as his proxy.

The letter was partly a recollection and restatement of some strange and humorous rules of life Brian has been sending to Neal each year from the time he was born.

"Never shave a cat" was one of those odd early admonitions. Another was "Never eat anything bigger than your head." Clearly, these were guidelines intended to steer a young person in the direction of physical caution and moderation in consumption, with a little smile along the way.

But Brian's letter to Neal also contained some serious and excellent advice, which I'm sure he won't mind my repeating:

> You stand at the juncture of your boyhood, enjoyable and sunny, and your manhood, which promises to be confusing and delightful.
>
> Remember that being spiritually rich consists solely of being gentle and merciful, of paying attention to people whether they're rich or poor, smart or stupid, cool or nerdesque, and of trying to see the holiness in things.

It's in hoops, your mother's smile, your father's roar, your sister's laughter. It's in trees and birds and teachers and music. Its often very hard to see; it's hard to spot in sadness and tragedy, for example. But it's there, too. Holiness wears different clothes every day.

Godparenting, it has been said by some, has fallen on hard times. Being a godparent today, in a time when family members have often moved far away from one another, is much more difficult than it used to be, to do, to keep up with.

The role of godparent *has* changed, there is no doubt. Now, at baptism and later, parents are in the forefront and godparents in the background. The chief responsibility for the spiritual training of a child lies with the child's parents, as it should.

But godparents still have vital roles to play in the spiritual development of their godchildren. They must serve as good examples of committed Catholic Christians. They need to keep in touch, and they need to be around regularly, to be available—even if at long distance—for talking, advising, and supporting.

Anyone who's been asked to be a godparent, and parents needing to select godparents, would do well to consult *Godparents* by Deacon Henry P. Libersat, Jr. A handbook for parents and godparents who "want to rediscover what it means to share the joys and responsibilities in the formation of young Christians," in the author's words, this book explores what it means to be a godparent today and offers good advice on selecting godparents and nurturing godchildren at every stage of life. It offers tips on how to maintain a long-distance relationship with a godchild, and how to avoid godparent guilt when you haven't kept in touch the way you should have.

Being a godparent, especially in today's society, demands

constant and considerable practice. It's like marriage, like being a good mother or father or grandparent. Like being a good son or daughter—another role in life that requires regular attention, nourishing, and long-term care.

Come to think of it, being a good godparent is like growing a flower, but in somebody else's garden.

—J.D.

THE CHILDREN'S HOUR

Last Sunday at Mass we sat behind a young father and his three children: a boy just past five, a girl nearing four, and a younger girl, maybe two.

We wondered about their mother. Was she working, or ill, or maybe in the hospital having another baby, or maybe she isn't Catholic?

Whatever the reason for her absence, we sat in admiration of that young father. He was a big, strong fellow, maybe a policeman or fireman we thought, but remarkably gentle and patient and loving with his children, who, as you can imagine, were restless and wiggly, competing for his attention.

The baby wanted him to hold her all the time; the older girl wanted to stand in front of him on the kneeler; and the boy would have been happy to sit quietly beside him, but his sisters kept pushing in front of him and he had to insert his feet between them to maintain his space. And that led to more shoving and a little whining.

But the father never lost his patience. Somehow he kept them all reasonably quiet the whole time, talking with a smile to each at one time or another, holding the baby once in a while, and still paying attention and participating in the Mass.

How easy it would have been for this father to pass up going to Mass with his children altogether. "It's too much trouble," he might have said, "to get them all dressed and out on time. Have they all eaten and gone to the bathroom? How will I ever keep them under control? They'll just wiggle and whine, I'll be embarrassed, and the other people will be annoyed."

Thank God our young father didn't fall victim to any of those excuses, which we parents have all used at one time or another. All the rest of us in the church that day were the better for his coming and bringing them along. It was for us a wonderful extra part of the joyful celebration of the Mass.

Our pastor and his two associates (one a resident who works in the chancery) take turns celebrating the 9:30 Mass on Sundays as a special children's Mass, but it's quite different from the regimented children's Mass we all knew as children or as young parents raising our kids, with the children all packed into their own pews, squirming and smirking, under the watchful eyes and clackers of the sisters.

At our children's Mass, the pastor and the other priests invite all the children in the church to come forward and sit as a group gathered around the altar. When the priests started it some months ago, only a few children came forward, but as each week passes, more and more families are bringing their children to this Mass, and more and more kids come hurrying from every part of the church to join the celebrant on the steps.

The priest seats himself in front of the altar in a small chair, coming down to the children's level, humanizing himself, and the children arrange themselves around him, sitting on the steps and the front part of the sanctuary. Most of the kids come up alone, but some come with brothers or sisters, the older ones holding the little ones' hands. For the older children, who might have grown too sophisticated to go up by themselves, taking a little brother or sister along gives them a special status, and the younger ones, who might be afraid otherwise, go along more readily.

The kids quite naturally gather in a sort of semicircle, with the priest in the center, and it strikes me that this is a position and an occasion very Christlike in nature, for Jesus must often have taught like this, seated on a simple chair or on the ground, with the people all around him.

Because he is teaching children, the priest must simplify the lessons, couching his homily in clear, understandable language. That, plus the drama of the moment, helps all of us.

Often the homilist will use a graphic symbol or some other visual aid to get his message across. One priest used Halloween masks as props, and another time a blindfolded boy, and the rest of us learned it is better to follow someone leading us—as we follow Christ—than to be pushed from behind.

In a real sense, these children gathered around the priest for this teaching moment each week are ministers of the Mass, too. They help to make the Word more meaningful and the Mass more real and fulfilling for themselves and for all of us.

—J.D.

Our Fat Old Christmas Angel

Some years ago, one of our sons who has a puckish sense of humor fashioned a strange but lovable angel for our Christmas tree. It came to light not long ago when I was going through our box of Christmas decorations.

Traditional angels are sexless beings, as I understand it, and have no bodies, but our Christmas angel is definitely a guy, clearly an average male-type angel, and he definitely has a body.

He's sort of every angel, you might say—a little bit below average height and somewhat overweight, with much of his weight distributed in the wrong places, like most of us. His shoulders are narrower than his waist, and his legs seem too thick for his torso. He looks a lot older than he is.

Our angel has a big—no, not big: bulbous—nose, clearly in the Doyle tradition, our son, his creator, says. He has a thick black mustache, and his eyes are not quite lined up properly. He has three worry lines on his forehead and a bit of a cleft in his chin. Altogether not a very handsome angel, but he's ours.

Our angel has wings, of course, but they are not delicate and fluttering. They're big and heavy and flaring, and they cover his whole back, sort of like bat's wings.

Our angel originally came into being, in black and white, at Christmas in 1976. When Brian, his originator, married, his wife, Mary, colored the angel properly for posterity. He is wearing a maroon shirt (with a little identifying gold *a* on it), purple pants, white gloves, and striped wings. His face is sort of weathered and homely. His halo, his crowning glory, is also gold with pinkish stripes. It's a bit askew, though, and fits him like a floppy French beret.

As you can see, this is not your run-of-the-mill angel. We asked Brian why this angel was so different and so...well, human. He said he figured since no one had really seen an angel lately, his vision was probably as valid as anyone else's. Besides, he argued, there must be some imperfect angels, some with mustaches and beards, a little short in stature and gone to fat, maybe even with big noses and funny-looking ears. Can't argue with that, I guess.

Anyway, by family acclamation our angel has reigned over our Christmas tree for many years now, bringing a special kind of Christmas cheer to our house.

But he is only one of our family Christmas customs.

This Christmas Brian was at it again. He gathered his young nieces and nephews and his own daughter and with them created *The Doyle Chronicle,* a hand-drawn, one-page record of our Christmas events. His young girl and boy reporters went out all over the house and brought back sterling stories with gripping headlines like "Great Deal Going On at Doyle House!" "Diane Loves Tom!" "Jane's Favorite Book: Pooh!" "Betsy Has Arrived!" "Nana's Favorite Song: Amazing Grace!" And then there was the screamer headline "DISH-WASHER BUSTED; ALL MOURN!"

It was a clever and popular idea. We framed the page for posterity, and I think we'll be publishing *The Doyle Chronicle* again next year.

My wife always bakes a birthday cake with a candle for Baby Jesus—an idea we borrowed from Maryknoll. The infant rests on a bed of coconut in the center of the cake all through Christmas and for some days afterward. One year she didn't make the cake, figuring our children were too old for that sort of thing, but there arose such a clatter of complaint that two of our daughters-in-law had to whip up a Jesus birthday cake to get us back to tradition, fast.

For years I've been making a huge Christmas wreath, six

feet in diameter, cutting yew branches out back and weaving in lights so that we can hang our wreath outside to help light the neighborhood for the holidays. I hate doing the job but wouldn't think of not doing it.

And then there are the Christmas stockings still hung by the fireplace with care—one for each child and now one for each grandchild. We tried to drop that tradition too one year, but another howl arose. We've never since tried to interfere with any more Christmas customs.

Until this year. This year we were out West for Christmas and New Year's Eve with two of our sons and their families. All of our sons, with their wives and children, are making their own Christmas traditions now, as they should. So for the first time in years our angel stayed in his box. Maybe next year he'll take his place at the top of our tree again. And one year soon we will pass our fat old Christmas angel on to his creator and his colorist so that they can include him in their Christmases in years to come. The way it ought to be.

—J.D.

THE PRIEST WHO
DREAMED UP AN AIRPORT

I first met James P. Horan when he was a parish priest in the little village of Knock in County Mayo in west Ireland and he had two great ideas that were consuming him—one of which seemed improbable and the other quite impossible.

His improbable project was to get Pope John Paul II to come all the way from Rome to Knock to visit the Shrine of Our Lady of Knock at the parish church there—where the Blessed Mother appeared with Saint Joseph and Saint John the Evangelist in August of 1879—and to bless the new Basilica of Our Lady Queen of Ireland built in the mid-1970s.

The other idea, which nearly everyone except Father Horan agreed was impossible, was to get the Irish government to build a new airport at Knock, to bring pilgrims from all over the world to the shrine and to bring industry and jobs to the people of County Mayo, historically one of the poorest parts of Ireland.

On my first visit to Knock, with a group of Catholic journalists who were touring Ireland, the gracious and charming Father Horan, in a press briefing, told us—with lots of humor in his delivery and a steady twinkle in his eyes—of his grand plan to build a new airport at Knock.

He stressed the need for an airport, which would perform an economic miracle for Mayo, opening up the poor farm country of the west, bringing in new business, and creating new jobs. And, he also expected, an airport would bring about rapid increases in pilgrimages to the shrine and Mayo tourism.

It was hard for our skeptical American Catholic journalists to swallow the idea that such an airport would ever be seen on the bogland of Mayo. Reactions at that briefing ranged from surprised to shocked to disbelieving. It all seemed nothing more than a dream concocted by this chunky, charming, media-wise Irish parish priest to get some press coverage for his shrine.

But he told us that he had gotten some people in the Irish government interested in the project and that we should come back in a few years to see his airport. Despite our skepticism, we could tell that he was quite serious and determined about the project.

Obviously, he knew what he was talking about. The next time I went back to Knock, it was 1979—one hundred years after the apparition—and the parish priest, now Monsignor Horan, had accomplished his first, improbable project: getting the pope to come to Knock.

Our journalist tour group, which had covered the pope's visit to Dublin, where a million people went to see him in Phoenix Park, arrived in Knock the day after John Paul II's visit there. Monsignor Horan was tired but exultant, bushed but beaming, and full of joy at the pope's having come to bless the shrine and the new basilica.

Then he took us out to see the proof that his second, impossible project was about to happen. He boarded our tour bus one dreary morning in October and rode with us a few miles north of Knock, up a muddy road to the top of a bog hill, and there showed off his new airport's runway, which had just recently been poured.

The fog was thick but his smile was broad as he proudly told us construction would begin soon on the main terminal and other facilities. He had, indeed, against heavy odds, persuaded the Irish government and the Irish people that his airport was needed.

The last time I saw Monsignor Horan, in 1983, he was celebrating his fiftieth anniversary as a priest. He was his usual gracious self. At his residence-office complex, he came down to greet me and my wife and friends and talk a while, but he seemed worn out and not feeling well.

A couple of years later, I read in the papers that Horan International Airport had indeed opened—on October 25, 1985—six years after the pope's visit. A picture I have of Monsignor Horan that day shows him with his enormous charming smile and his arms thrown wide, welcoming the world to Knock and to his airport.

Now, I understand, air traffic is increasing regularly at Horan Airport, duty-free sales at the terminal are doing well, and regular transatlantic flights from New York and Boston are being talked about. Some day, I think, Horan International will be a big success.

Monsignor James P. Horan died a few years ago, at Lourdes in France, after taking one of the first flights out of Horan International Airport. It was a fitting way for God to welcome him home after his wonderful work at Knock.

—J.D.

CLOSING OUR SCHOOL,
AND STARTING ANEW

Our parish elementary school finally closed its doors in June, after recent years of struggling to survive with fewer and fewer students—but also after forty-one years of happy and fruitful existence and service. One can only wonder what our parish will be like without the school, around which so much of parish and family life revolved for all those years.

Of course, the church building itself is the main gathering place of a parish, where the central mystery of the Eucharist is celebrated, where we live our faith and come together with one another and with God. But a parish school becomes in fact the second center of a parish fortunate enough to have one—the key place in which we build parish community.

The parish school was often the reason we Catholics selected the place we lived. Back in the '50s, after inspecting other towns and other parishes, we chose our village because the big, new Catholic school was here. We bought the house we occupy because it was only a short walk for our children to the parish school.

We Doyles have been involved in almost the entire life of our parish school—thirty-seven of its forty-one years. All our five children went through Curé of Ars School, and now—coming full circle—our youngest son teaches there.

And over the years, as our children were involved in school activities, we also got involved and came to know and esteem other parents and their children. Now, years later, we still count as friends many of those people we worked with and got to know through the school, parish dances and parties in the school, and school sports and scouting.

Later on, the school was the reason other parishioners became involved in running bingo or the annual parish carnival, because carnival and bingo money was desperately needed to offset the drain the school became on our parish budget.

At a much more inspiring level, our school was a major influence, I am sure, on fifteen young parish men who went on to be ordained priests over a period of twenty years or so—a remarkable record and a great tribute to the school and the sisters and, later, lay teachers who staffed it, and the priests and parents who supported it.

The school was originally staffed by the Sisters of Saint Dominic of Amityville—dedicated women—some truly gifted and some not, and a few who should never have been teachers at all. They left when their numbers eroded in the turbulent '70s, but the parish decided to carry on, raised tuition, and hired a lay faculty. And the school survived another twenty years.

But now the end has come. Our school is closed, but it continues in a new form as part of a regional school that four parishes in our area will support and share. With the new regional school opening this week—named for and dedicated to America's holiest teacher, Saint Elizabeth Ann Seton— a new phase of our parish life has begun.

At the Mass and sad ceremony officially closing the old school, the old banner of Curé of Ars School was happily joined to the new banner of St. Elizabeth Ann Seton School. Our son Tom, who has been appointed assistant principal of the new school, read those famous verses from Ecclesiastes:

> For everything there is a season, and a time for
>   every matter under heaven:
> a time to be born, and a time to die;

a time to plant, and a time to pluck up what is
  planted;
a time to kill, and a time to heal;
a time to break down, and a time to build up...
  (3:1–3).

It's time now to fashion a new school for new generations, and time to ask God's blessings on the new school and its students and faculty, on the new work to be done and the people who will do it. It's time also to thank God—and all those who helped make it work—for our old school and all it meant to us and the people of our parish.

—J.D.

MY FRIEND BIG PADRE NORMANDO

My very big friend Norman J. Muckerman, a Redemptorist priest who used to be editor of the *Liguorian* magazine, has published a book telling about the marvelous work of Redemptorist priests and brothers from his St. Louis province who have been serving in the Amazon River valley of Brazil for the past fifty years. It's called *Redemptorists on the Amazon: The First Fifty Years.*

His new book may not make the bestseller lists. It may not even have a wide distribution, but it is well worth reading because it's an absorbing account of how one part of just one of the Church's many mission-sending societies accomplished its excellent mission work, in one part of the world, over the past half-century.

Padre Normando, as he was known in Brazil, writes well, as he records carefully and in detail—with names, dates, and places—how the Redemptorists' Amazonian mission effort was conceived and carried out. And he is honest and frank in relating how their evangelization work faltered in the years following the Second Vatican Council—but also how it is growing anew now, with more native clergy taking charge.

Father Muckerman's little book is an excellent history of a great period in the Church's efforts to bring the faith to people in places far from Europe and North America. It will be an important record for future historians who tell the story of American Catholic missions in the twentieth century.

Father Muckerman's hundreds of friends call him Big Norm, or the Big M, because he is quite tall (six foot six or so) and imposing in stature. In fact, he often calls himself that. "Have no fear," he says, "Big Norm is here."

In the old days, when he was just ordained and went out to the missions in Amazonia in 1944, he was a lean, athletic young priest. These days he is, like many of us, no longer very lean, but his size makes him all the more dominating a figure, with a big, booming voice, a warm smile, and a hearty, friendly style. Often he will wrap a big bear hug around a friend to show his affection. He is a holy and pastoral priest, and a loving person.

Over the many years I worked with him at the Catholic Press Association—on committees and the board of directors and for the three wonderful years he was president—I marveled at how open and gracious he was, always, to everyone he met. Wherever we went, I would soon find him in friendly conversation—with people he encountered on airplanes, with desk clerks in hotels, with restaurant staff, with children we met on study tours we took together, or in golf foursomes.

He was the perfect president for the Catholic Press Association—a chief executive of style and stature who called attention to the Catholic press by his physical being, his friendly manner, his professionalism, and his special gift as a great joke- and storyteller.

He was also a very spiritual leader—always trying to relate the daily drudgery of Catholic publishing to the transcendent purpose for which we were all laboring. Even today he is looked upon as a spiritual leader within the Catholic press: he was asked to give a talk on spirituality in the Catholic press at the one hundredth anniversary of the Franciscans' *St. Anthony Messenger* magazine.

Big Norm recently celebrated the fifty-fifth anniversary of his ordination as a priest, and the fiftieth anniversary of the parish he established in Belem, Brazil. He came back to turn his attention to the Redemptorists' publishing work—another form of the preaching mission that is their principal focus. First he worked in the business end of the *Liguorian* and then stepped in as editor—and was a huge success at that also, as you might expect.

Now he is retired, and it is appropriate that attention be paid and thanks be given to Big Norm. His new book is a tribute to his energy and continued dedication to the work he undertook more than fifty years ago and to his steadfast priesthood in the service of the Lord and the people of God.

—J.D.

"A Street-Fighter for the Poor"

A great holy priest died a few weeks ago in Denver. His life was so compassionate, so inspiring—and so dedicated to the poor, the hungry, and the homeless, whom Christ loved and told us to love—that one can't help believing he was a saint among us.

Formally and officially he was Monsignor Charles Bert Woodrich, but this wonderful priest who personified what a priest today ought to be—"a living witness of the priest called to serve," the archbishop of Denver called him—was never formal and rarely official. I never heard him called anything but Woody.

My wife and I came to know and love him in the eleven years he was the brilliant editor of the *Denver Catholic Register* and, for a time, a member of the board of directors of the Catholic Press Association, of which I was executive editor.

He was a simple, direct, no-nonsense man. When he telephoned me, he would usually just bark, "Doyle, this is Woodrich." He couldn't tolerate cant or pomposity, dishonesty or phoniness, whether in priests or laypeople.

He was impressed by true holiness, though. One of his happiest moments was the time Mother Teresa visited Denver and he was asked to drive her around the archdiocese. He was also impressed by young journalists who worked in the Catholic press for low pay because they thought they should be doing God's work in the media.

Charlene Scott, writing the story of his death in the *Register*, called him "Denver's patron saint of the hungry and homeless and the city's most famous priest...a street-fighter for the poor."

When Woody died, on a Sunday in November, from a terrible asthma attack and, probably, the effects of diabetes and emphysema, from which he'd been suffering for years, his death was big news: a local TV station flashed a news bulletin about it, and the next day the two Denver daily papers gave over their front pages and many inside pages to the man they called "champion of the homeless...friend to the poor."

Woody was born in Buffalo and went to college back East, then worked in New York with Batten, Barton, Durstine & Osborne advertising agency for a while. It was there, I am sure, that he refined the natural talents he had for advertising and promotion, and his keen instincts for knowing how the good work the Church was doing could be promoted.

He decided to become a priest and chose Denver, partly because he thought it would help his asthma, from which he suffered all his life. He was ordained there in 1953, at age thirty. He worked fourteen years in an inner-city parish and two years as a hospital chaplain. "He emerged," Charlene Scott wrote in the obituary, "as a blunt, tough-talking, fearless defender of the downtrodden."

Then he became pastor of another downtown Denver parish, Holy Ghost Church, and ran a sandwich line there for hungry people six days a week. One day, in the wicked Colorado winter of 1981–82, he looked out the window at the people huddled against the bitter wind and below-zero cold on the streets and suddenly was struck by the idea to open his church to them.

That first winter, sixty people spent the freezing nights sleeping on the pews of Holy Ghost Church. "You can't pray to the Lord and reject the ones He loved the most," Woody told his parishioners.

Then he persuaded the archbishop that the archdiocese

should remodel an unused high school into a full-time shelter with sections for men, women, and families. It was called Samaritan Shelter. News about it spread across the country (helped along by Woody's sense of promotion and media contacts). He and his idea were featured in *People* magazine, *Time, Newsweek, USA Today,* and on ABC's *Nightline.*

Under Woody's urging, the archdiocese built another new and larger facility—the first shelter in the United States constructed specifically for the homeless—which now cares for 350 people each day.

When he died, the papers were full of praise for Woody from his fellow priests, friends, city and state officials, parishioners, and the poor people he knew so well. But the best comment was that of Sharon Brisnehan, a Samaritan House employee.

"I'm not sad for Father Woody," she said. "It's a great day for him. He is right where he should be. He is with his Lord."

—J.D.

Reaching Out, Helping Others

I think the most important and impressive activity in the life of the Church today—because it is so truly Christlike—is the work of the parish outreach programs that are now, thank God, proliferating throughout the land.

In parishes here and all across the country, the hungry, the hurting, and the homeless are being fed, clothed, sheltered, and comforted by thousands of laypeople, priests, and sisters. Their inspiring labor imitates the work Christ did and would do if he were here today.

Focusing for the moment on parish outreach programs takes nothing away from the great humanitarian work of Catholic Relief Services, the Catholic Worker movement, Covenant House, the St. Vincent de Paul Society, and the mission orders and societies active overseas and here at home. But I submit that parish outreach programs are Christlike because they are one-on-one, face-to-face, serving people in our own neighborhoods. They feed the hungry, the poor, and the troubled most of us don't even know exist in our own towns and villages.

Our outreach office gets a lot of support from our parishioners, who volunteer to help out in lots of ways, confronting and solving hundreds of problems parish people have, week in, week out. There are friendly visitors who go regularly to see homebound clients—to talk, yes, but mostly to listen. There is a cadre of drivers who take sick people to doctors and hospitals; someone even drove one lady once to a beauty parlor because having her hair done was just the psychological medicine she really needed. There are people who come to help on their lunch breaks and one nurse who helps out on her day off.

Our parishioners also come through in providing the means with which the volunteers can help those in need. Once a month there is a food collection, and on that Sunday the outreach office is inundated with bags of groceries. This allows the outreach office to provide food for families in our parish who just couldn't make it without this help. Our outreach volunteers feed one poor homeless guy who sleeps in his car; they had to give him a can opener because he exists mostly on food from cans and plastic containers. And every so often the outreach office schedules a Mass of Anointing and a luncheon for the chronically ill and the fragile aged.

When outreach volunteers ask for used clothing, the place is stuffed with cartons of clothes people bring in; it takes days to sort it all out. Our outreach people have recently located and given away some nearly new first Communion suits and dresses that were needed; provided some business-style dresses for a lady client who just got a new job; and last winter collected and distributed warm coats and hats. Just last week they found somebody to donate a used wheelchair for a woman who broke her leg.

Often, the volunteers tell me, people just drop by and leave money—sometimes bills, sometimes coins. One time somebody brought in a big jar full of quarters, nickels, dimes, and pennies. Cleaned and counted, they added up to an $82 donation.

Our parish has also turned our former convent into a home for a group of frightened young women who have rejected abortion and are having their babies alone. Run as part of the outreach program, it is called Regina Residence.

The young ladies often come over to the outreach office to help out. The other day several of them were going through a big bag of baby clothes that had just come in. It was like a mini baby shower, my wife said. They were choosing outfits for their babies, oohing and aahing over the cute clothes, speculating if they would have a boy or girl, talking about names they might give them.

One of the best new ideas for Christmastime is the Giving Tree, which our parish outreach office has been using now for several years with great success, and which I see many other parishes in different parts of the country using as well. I have no idea who first thought up the idea of the Giving Tree. I wish I knew.

The way it works, at least in our parish, is that our outreach people put up a big Christmas tree in the back of our church, and volunteers hang hundreds of colored construction-paper tags all over the tree. Each tag describes a person for whom a gift is needed—a boy, six, for example; or a senior man; or a single mother; or a girl, twelve—but no personal names are ever used, of course. Sometimes the tags ask for specific gifts—a sweater for an infant, maybe, or a warm jacket for a girl of three—things like that. Young people preparing for confirmation do the tags as part of their service project, a nice by-product of the process.

For two Sundays in Advent the tree stands there, adorned with the gift tags, and parishioners are invited to take a tag and buy or make the listed gift. There's always an enthusiastic response, and the tags go quickly. Then on one of the Sundays right before Christmas all the gifts come back; they must be wrapped, with the original tag on the outside. All day that Sunday they are stacked around the tree, and then the outreach office takes them and gives them to our needy parish families.

The special genius of the Giving Tree is that it's a dramatic and efficient way to channel a lot of our good feeling at Christmas into action.

Even in our comfortable suburban parish, and certainly in

urban parishes, there are many hurting people—some without employment, without money for gifts or clothes or toys for their children, and in some cases even some without food for Christmas meals. Parishioners of good heart and good circumstances get a chance to help some less fortunate neighbors they might never otherwise know about or ever meet personally.

A critic might say the impersonal nature of anonymous Giving Tree giving leaves a lot to be desired. But doing a good deed anonymously is better than not doing it at all, and maybe a lot better for the soul than doing it with fanfare.

Our outreach office and program is fairly small and modest; there are some really big shows elsewhere in our diocese and around the country, I know. But small or large, these programs and these people are doing quiet, stunning, prayerful, Christlike work.

—J.D.

About the Authors

James Doyle, executive director of the Catholic Press Association from 1958 to 1988, is a columnist for *Catholic New York,* the newspaper of the archdiocese of New York. His articles, essays, and stories have appeared in *U.S. Catholic, Catholic Digest, The Critic, The Priest, View,* and *The Long Island Catholic,* among other publications. He is the author of *Our Parish Council Is Alive and Working!* (Liguori Publications, 1969), and he was a contributor to *If I Were Pope* (Thomas More Press, 1987). In 1984 he was named a Knight of Saint Gregory the Great by Pope John Paul II, for service to the Church and to the Catholic Press. That year he was also named alumnus of the year by his alma mater, Queens College of the City University of New York. He and his wife, Ethel Clancey Doyle, live in Merrick, New York.

Brian Doyle is the editor of *Portland* at the University of Portland, in Oregon. His essays, stories, and poems have appeared in *America, Ar Mhuin na Muice, The American Scholar, Commonweal, The Critic, First Things, Oregon Birds, U.S. Catholic,* and *Yankee,* among other publications. His essay "Pointing East" is included in the book *Thoughts of Home* (Hearst Books, 1995). He and his wife, Mary Miller Doyle, an artist, have three children and live in Lake Oswego, Oregon.